Excel
Basic Skills

Reading and Comprehension

Years 1–2
Ages 6–8

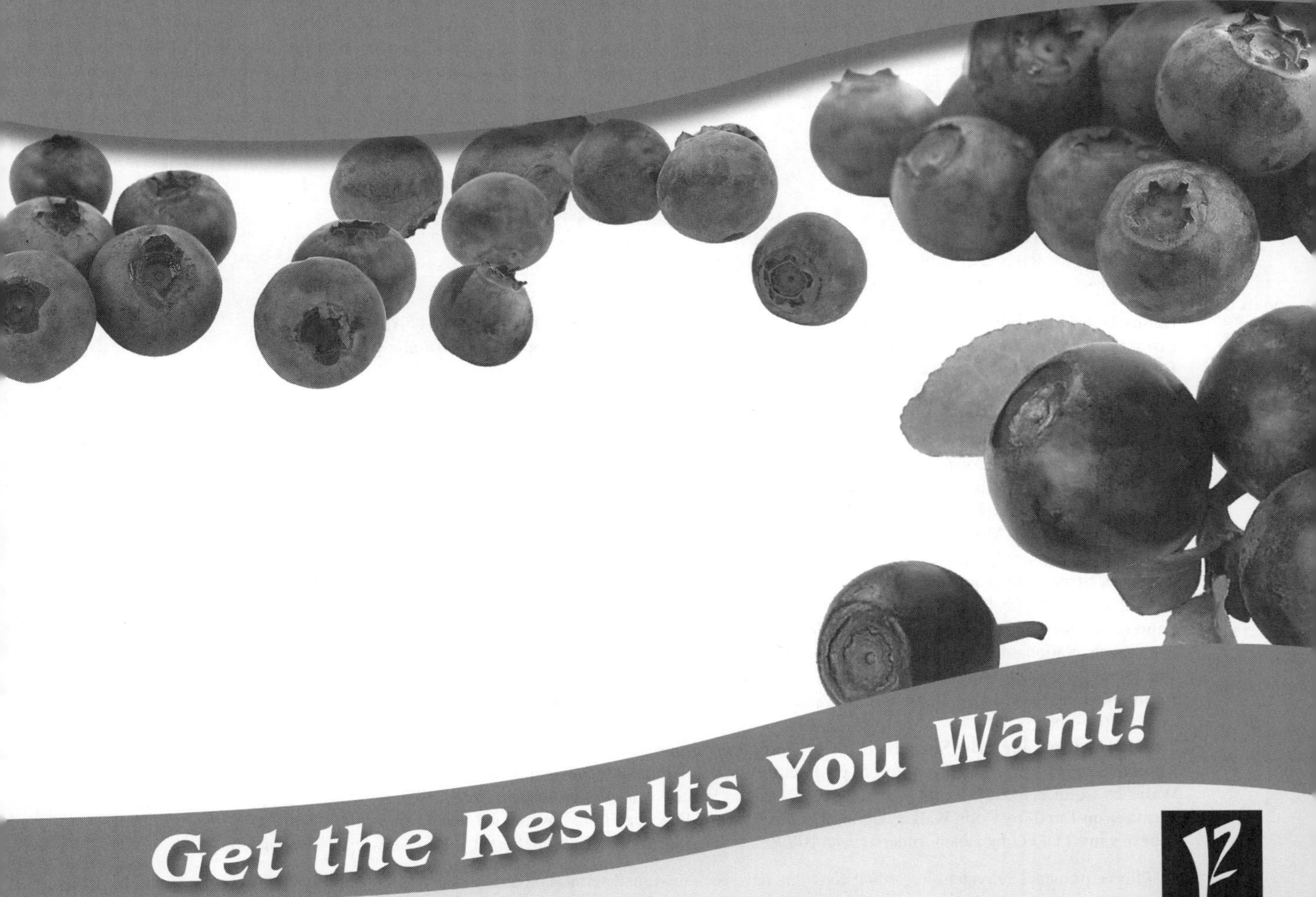

Get the Results You Want!

Alan Horsfield

Reprinted 2000, 2001, 2002, 2003, 2004, 2005, 2006, 2007, 2008 (twice), 2009 (twice), 2010, 2011, 2012 (twice)

Updated in 2013 for the Australian Curriculum

Reprinted 2014, 2016, 2017 (twice), 2019, 2020, 2021, 2022, 2023, 2024

ISBN 978 1 86441 340 3

Pascal Press
PO Box 250
Glebe NSW 2037
(02) 9198 1748
www.pascalpress.com.au

Publisher: Vivienne Joannou
Project editor: Mark Dixon
Text design and typesetting by Scriptorium Desktop Publishing Pty Ltd
Additional typesetting by Grizzly Graphics (Leanne Richters)
Cover by Dizign Pty Ltd
Printed by Vivar Printing/Green Giant Press

Acknowledgements

Elaine Horsfield of EJH Talent Promotion P/L for support, research and proofreading
Loren, Bindi and Holly for the use of their photographs
Val Andrews for selected artwork (chocolate frog and sandcastle)
Kylie Lowson for professional assistance

Danny Dolphin's Holiday by Gordon Winch and Gregory Blaxell. Blake Education, Glebe NSW Australia 1997
From the Land of Ikaros by Petro Alexiou, Spectrum Series, Harcourt Brace Jovanovich, Australia 1989
Ideas About Space by Colin Walker, Concept Science, Set C, Harcourt Brace Jovanovich, Australia 1989
I Keep Three Wishes Ready by Annette Wynne from **All Through the Day** J. P. Lippencott Co., 1932
It's so Hard to be Perfect by B. W. Shearer, NSW School Magazine **Countdown** Vol 78 No. 9 Oct 1993
Kzot the Amazing Robot by Jan Weeks, Spectrum series, Harcourt Brace Jovanovich, Australia 1989
Light by Colin Walker, Concept Science, Set E, Harcourt Brace Jovanovich, Australia 1991
Living on Earth by Colin Walker, Concept Science Set C, Harcourt Brace Jovanovich 1989
Mice by Rose Fyleman. Reprinted with permission of The Society of Authors as the literary representative of the estate of Rose Fyleman.
Numbat Run! by Jill Morris, Spectrum series, Harcourt Brace Jovanovich, Australia 1989
The Old Ship by Gordon Winch and Gregory Blaxell, Blake Education, Glebe NSW Australia 1997
The Park Street Playground by Joy Cowley. Published by Wendy Pye Ltd. Available from Sunshine Books, 433 Wellington Street, Clifton Hill VIC 3068. Fax (03) 9482 2416.
Pandas by Christine A Deacon, Spectrum series, Harcourt Brace Jovanovich, Australia 1989
Pet Search. National Pet Search P/L Putney, NSW Australia, Ph 9809 6211.
The Picnic by Dorothy Aldis from **Hop, Skip and Jump** by Dorothy Aldis, Minton, Balch & Co. 1934, 1961
Robot Walk by Joy Cowley. Published by Wendy Pye Ltd. Available from Sunshine Books, 433 Wellington Street, Clifton Hill VIC 3068. Fax (03) 9482 2416.
Thunk The Dinosaur's Big Surprise by Lisby Gore, The Custom Book Co., 15B Penryhyn Ave Beecroft NSW 2119 (out of print).
Upon the Beach by Ilo Orleans from **I See a Poem**, Whitman Publishing Division, Racine Wisconsin 1968
Water by Colin Walker, Concept Science, Set F, Harcourt Brace Jovanovich, Australia 1991
Weather on Earth by Colin Walker, Concept Science, Set C, Harcourt Brace Jovanovich, 1989
Where's my Ticket? by Helen Anderson and Bill Reinholdt, Spectrum series, Harcourt Brace Jovanovich, 1989 Australia

All efforts to contact individuals regarding copyright have been made and permission acknowledged where applicable. Apologies to authors for accidental infringement where copyright has been untraceable. The publishers would appreciate any information on accurate copyright details.

Contents

To Parents and Teachers

Comprehension of text involves bringing meaning to written (and spoken) language. It is more than the reading of printed words. The meaning of words and the context in which they exist, along with punctuation and writing style, all contribute to the comprehension of a specific piece of text. By experiencing a range of text types the child is more able to find the meaning in a given text.

When the student completes the exercises in this book he or she will have worked through a number of question types from a variety of text types and practised a variety of skills.

This book begins with a list of sight words children should be able to recognise without hesitation. This is followed by a review of basic reading skills and exercises using a variety of passages (text types). These focus on developing the student's skill with particular question types. The book is structured so that if the student has a weakness or a 'gap' in a particular comprehension skill then the student can be directed to exercises that provide him or her with practice in that skill. Other passages can be used for revision purposes. With the help of an adult, the student will be able to focus on those skills that are appropriate.

The first text in many sections is intended to lead the student through a number of questions based upon a specific skill. Notes for parents and teachers are provided where background information will help the adult guide the student through various exercises. A full set of answers is provided in the middle of the book.

This book uses a range of text types so that the student will feel confident in a variety of situations. Text types are usually broken into two broad types. Within each group are numerous varieties — some are listed below.

Literary texts include narratives (novels/stories), poetry and (drama) scripts.

Factual texts include explanations, expositions, information reports, recounts and procedures.

As you can see, the list is quite long. It is important that students develop comprehension skills from a variety of text types. Many types of writing overlap.

In most classroom situations different comprehension skills can be developed from the same piece of text. Comprehension skills are interdependent.

Questions types include questions that require the following:

- true or false responses (yes or no)
- multiple-choice responses
- short-answer responses
- full-sentence answers
- matching skills
- sentence completing
- cloze skills (filling in blanks)
- sequencing skills
- open-ended responses
- giving reasons
- language knowledge
- labelling skills.

Level of Difficulty

The first section of this book provides some revision of those basic skills learned in Year 1 and developed throughout Year 2. Some more difficult texts, at the end of selected sections, are included to challenge the more able students. It is suggested that if younger students have difficulty with any exercise then it should be left and attempted at a later stage. As many Year 2 students are going through a period of rapid physical, social and intellectual growth such passages will provide extension exercises. They will provide preparation for the more formal work that the student will encounter in middle and upper primary.

It is suggested that students should give full-sentence answers unless directed otherwise. This helps the student focus on the intent of the question. Sufficient space is allowed for such answers.

Good luck!

Alan Horsfield

Basic Sight Word Vocabulary

There are a number of basic sight word lists around. This one (adapted from a Dolch list) is popular with many teachers of students learning to read.

It is suggested that parents use the list as a check list. When the student recognises the word without hesitation, give the word a tick or highlight it. This will provide students with a means of recording their progress.

The use of flash cards can be helpful in teaching the basic sight list. It is also a useful form of revision.

Remember: many of these basic sight words cannot be 'sounded out'. They are not spelled phonetically.

List 1	List 2	List 3	List 4	List 5
and	at	all	an	about
are	away	am	after	find
boy	bib	around	as	gave
can	blue	black	be	got
come	down	but	brown	has
funny	for	by	cold	its
go	good	call	did	know
he	green	came	ever	let
is	have	do	fly	live
jump	here	eat	from	made
like	in	fast	girl	many
little	man	get	give	may
look	me	going	had	new
my	it	home	help	now
of	not	into	her	over
play	on	make	him	put
red	one	no	his	around
run	ran	old	if	school
said	saw	out	she	so
says	three	was	some	soon
see	too	we	shop	ten
the	up	will	to	that
this	watch	yellow	who	under
to	you	yes	woman	your

List 6	List 7	List 8	List 9	List 10
about	because	brother	best	baby
again	been	buy	better	daughter
always	before	draw	both	far
any	bring	drink	clean	house
ask	children	even	cut	hurt
ate	done	fall	eight	kind
cannot	every	grow	five	laugh
could	goes	hold	four	Mr
does	mother	hot	full	Mrs
father	much	just	light	own
first	must	keep	myself	right
found	never	only	off	seven
how	once	pull	pick	sing
long	open	show	please	sister
or	our	sit	pretty	sleep
them	say	small	read	something
then	take	their	shall	son
they	tell	these	six	start
walk	three	think	today	than
went	upon	those	try	together
were	us	very	use	warm
what	want	where	well	wash
when	wish	which	why	water
with	would	work	write	white

It is suggested that parents add words that are especially relevant to the child's home, school or community.

My Own List

Using Basic Sight Words

1. Colour these boxes the right colour.

brown	blue	black	green	white

2. Write the number in the box above each word.

two	one	seven	four	ten

3. Draw the picture in the box above each word.

school	girl	man	water	baby

4. Colour the boxes which have words that you know.

them	better	myself	read	something
who	take	their	because	ever
they	woman	round	there	wash
please	three	think	today	daughter
under	upon	those	have	together

5. Write the name for each picture in the box.

Alphabetical Order

1. Can you complete the alphabet in this grid? Start at A and finish at Z.

A						
	I					
			R			
		X				

2. Join the dots. Start at A and finish at Z.

A W E L H

2. What did you draw when you joined the dots?
(The letters in the bubbles will help.)
A ____________ . Colour it.

Alphabetical order is sometimes called 'A, B, C' order or dictionary order. We can arrange words in alphabetical order. Words starting with A come before words that start with B.

1. In each line, colour the box with the word that comes first using alphabetical order.

mother	brother	sister	father	aunty
car	scooter	bike	ferry	helicopter
elephant	kangaroo	zebra	monkey	lion

2. Write the numbers 1 to 5 to show the alphabetical order of these three lists of words.

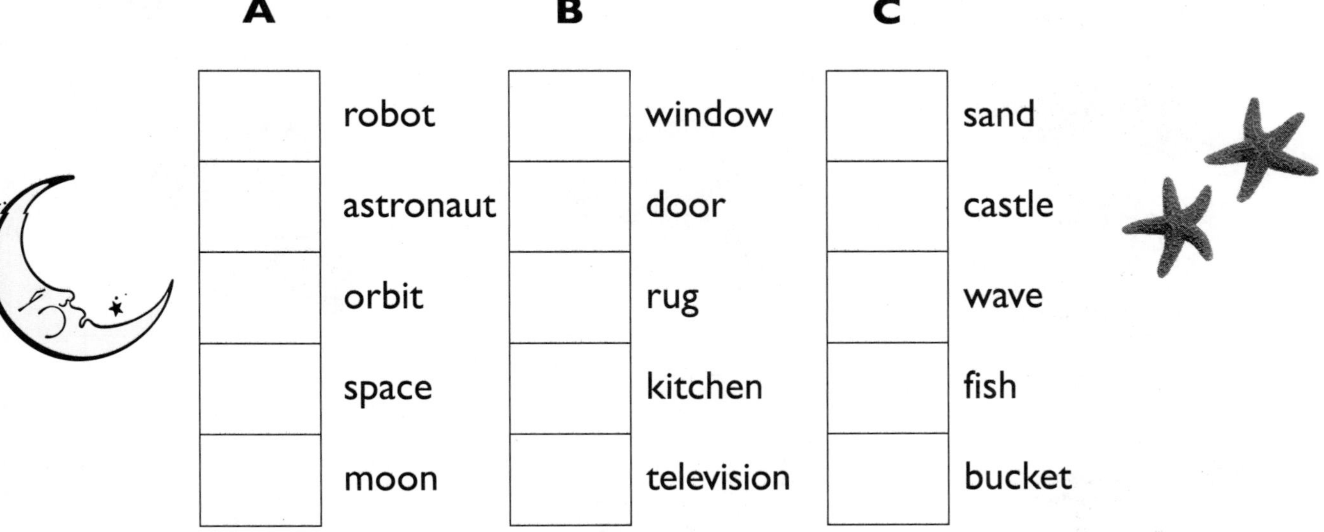

	A		B		C
	robot		window		sand
	astronaut		door		castle
	orbit		rug		wave
	space		kitchen		fish
	moon		television		bucket

3. Draw a line from one box to the next to show the alphabetical order of the words. Start with the word in the shaded box.
When you've joined the boxes, write a word in the empty box. Make it the last word in the order.

START

bottle	rabbit	weather
flag	house	

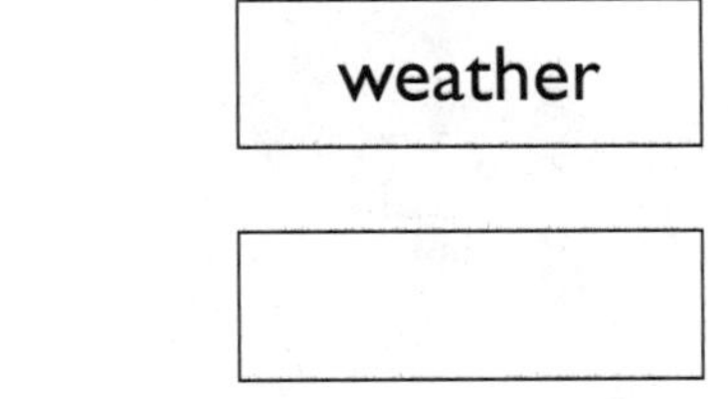

Recognising Initial Sounds

Look at each picture. Say its name and listen to the first sound of each word. Draw a circle around the letter with the same sound.

1.

a
b
c

2.

j
k
l

3.

s
t
u

4.

d
e
f

5.

m
n
o

6.

v
w
x

7.

g
h
i

8.

p
q
r

9.

y
z
a

Try these ones. They are a little harder.

10.

bl
br
dr

11.

cl
cr
st

12.

fl
sp
th

13.

sn
pl
ch

14.

sh
dr
gr

15

sl
pr
fr

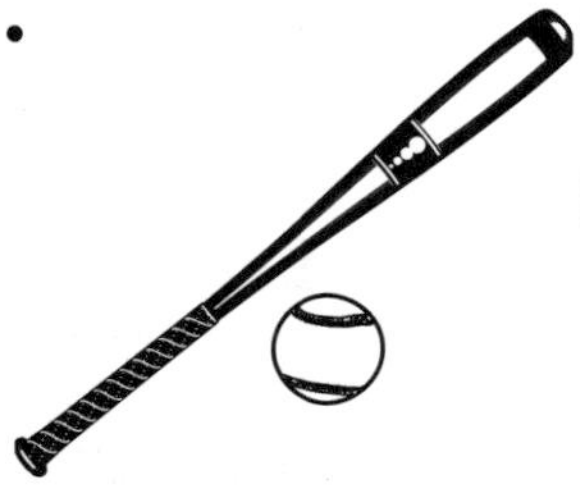

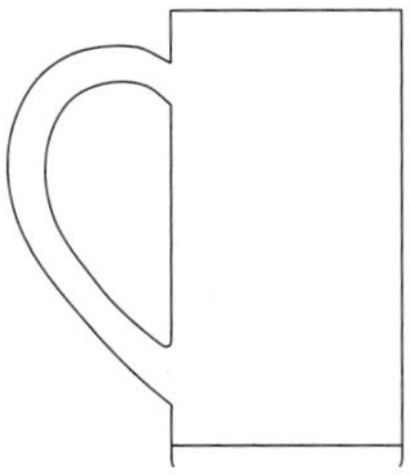

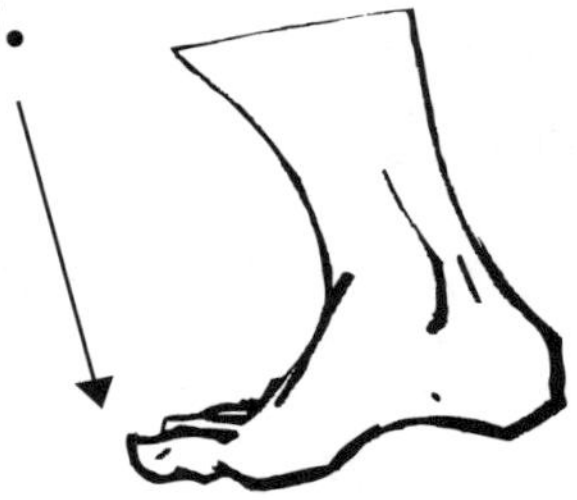

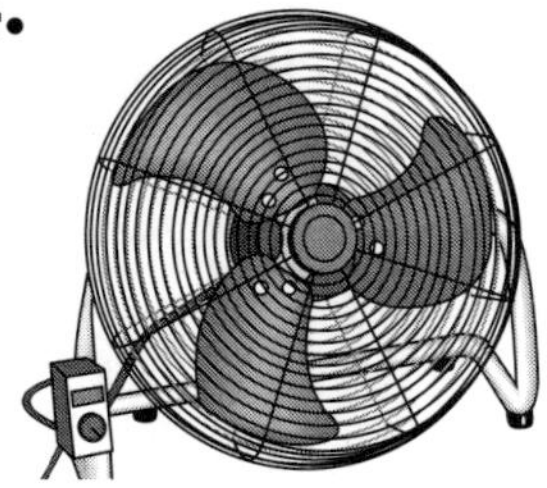

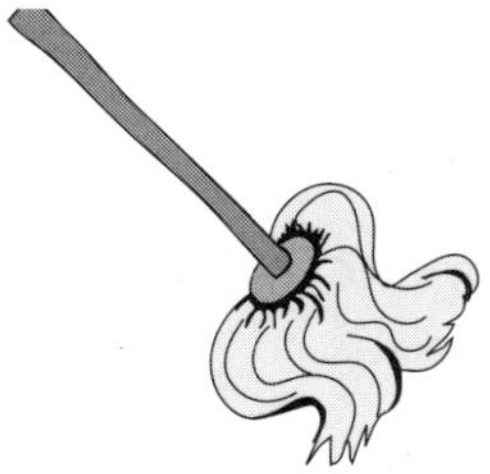

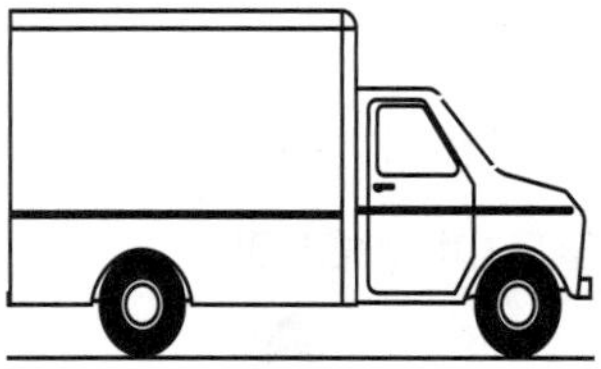

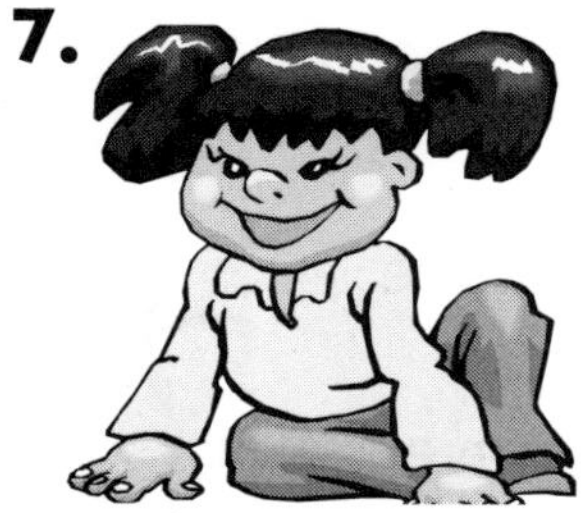

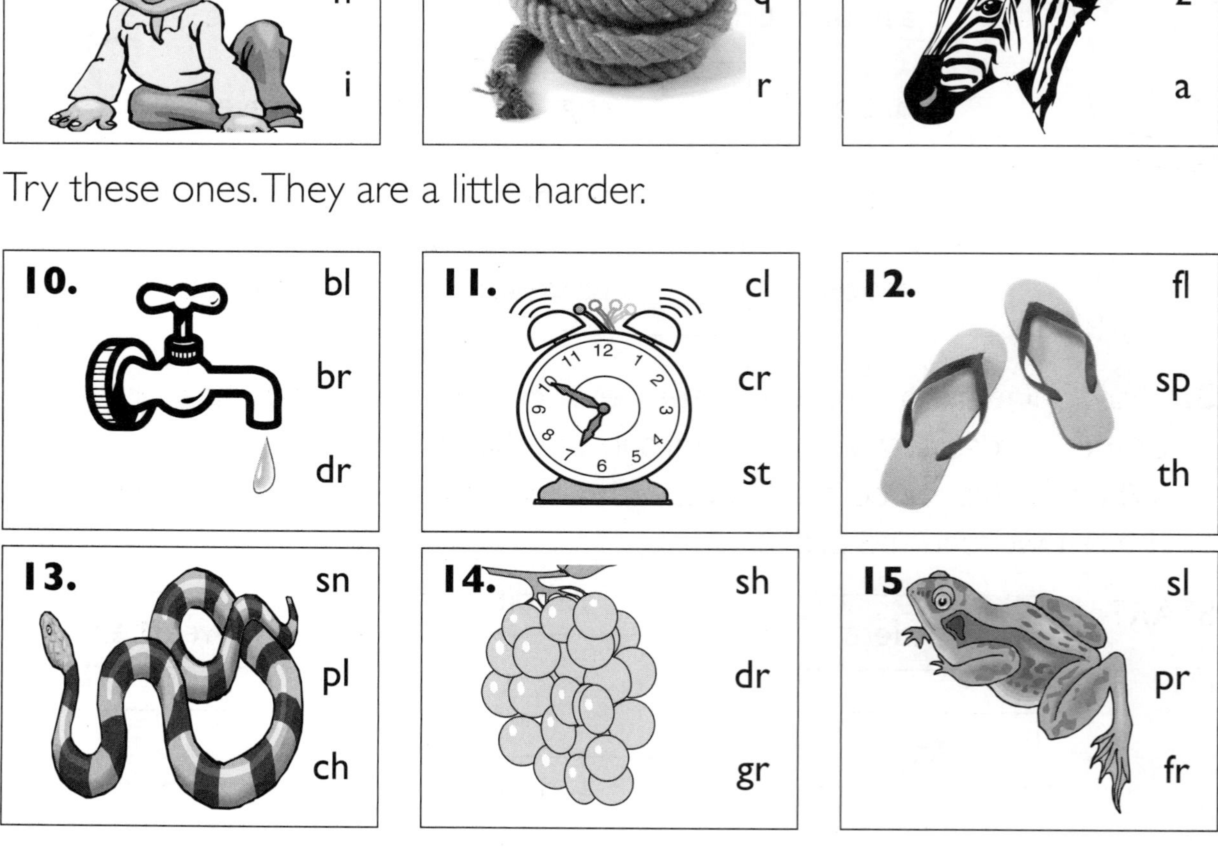

Recognising Final Sounds

Look at each picture. Say its name and listen to the last sound of each word. Draw a circle around the letter with the same sound.

1. 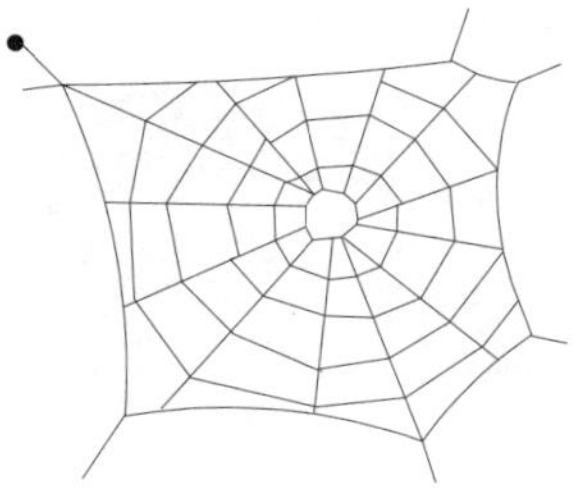 a b c
2.  j k l
3.  s t u
4.  d e f
5.  m n o
6. v w x
7. 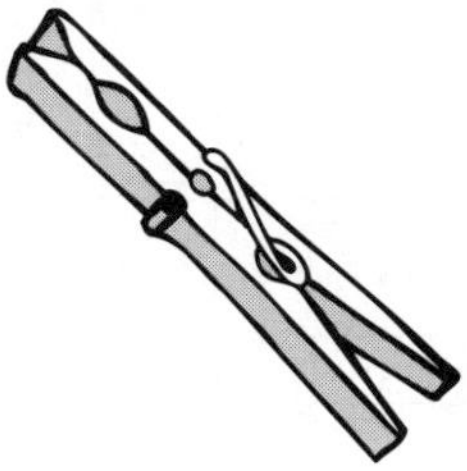 g h i
8.  p q r
9.  z b d

Try these ones. They are a little harder.

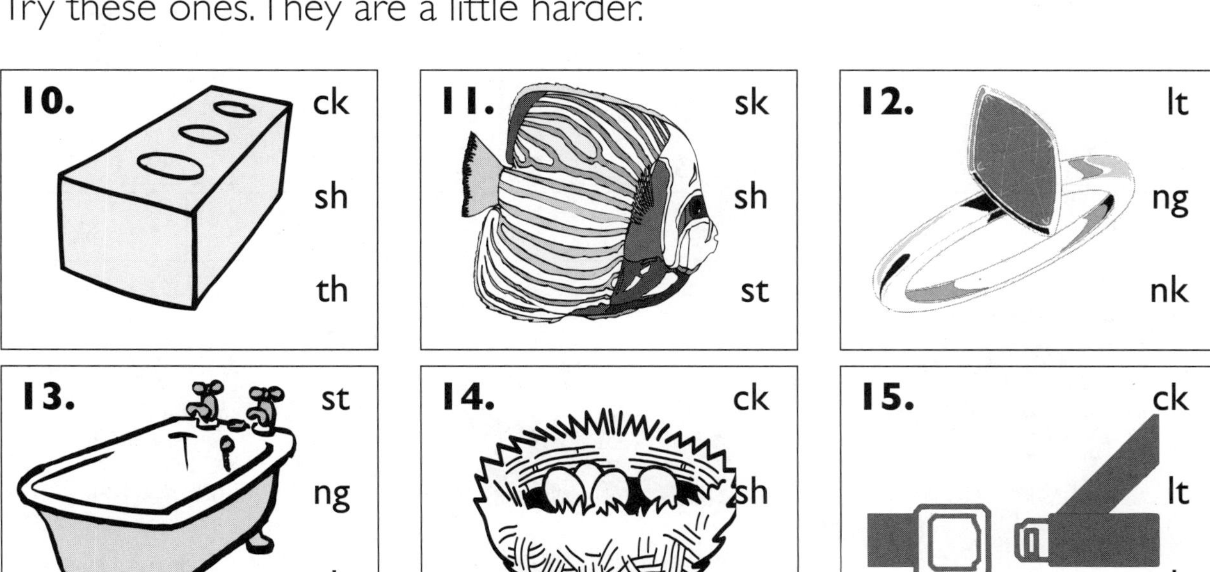

10. ck sh th
11. sk sh st
12. lt ng nk
13. st ng th
14. ck sh st
15. ck lt sk

Spelling with Blends

Look at each picture. Say its name.
Choose the correct letters from one of the boxes under the picture to complete the word. Write the letters in the spaces.

1.
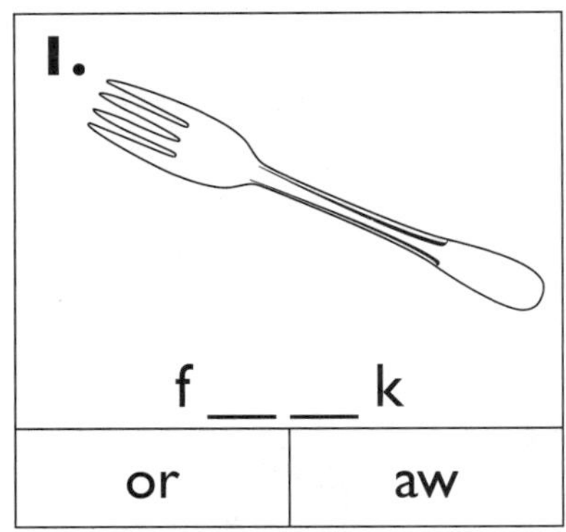

f ___ ___ k

or	aw

2.
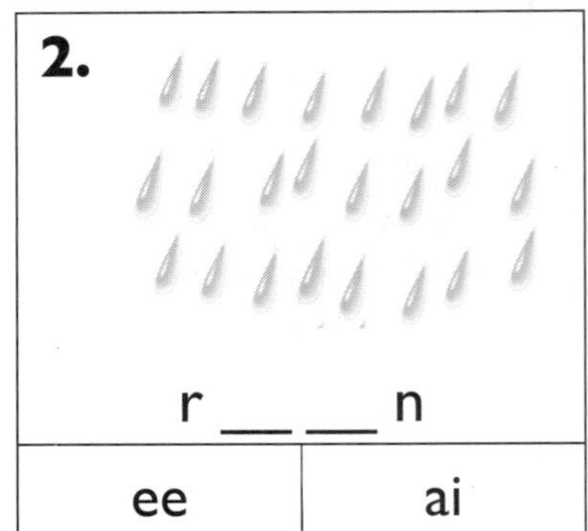

r ___ ___ n

ee	ai

3.
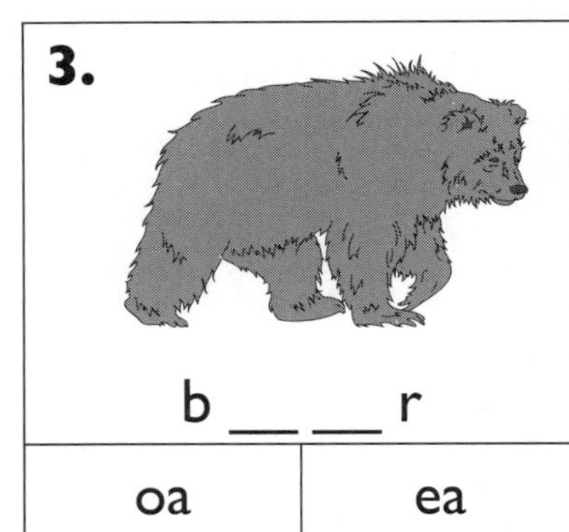

b ___ ___ r

oa	ea

4.
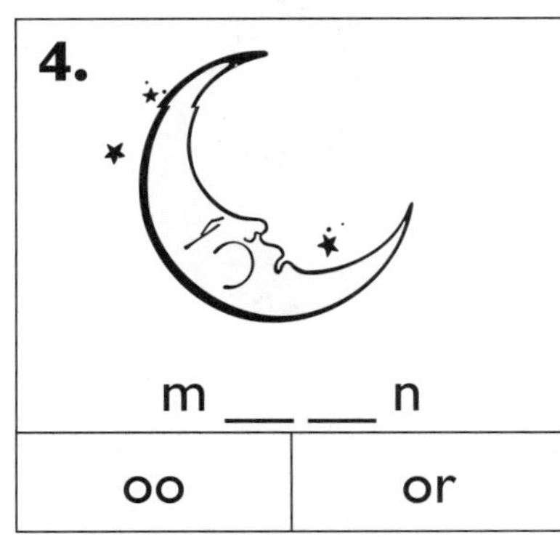

m ___ ___ n

oo	or

5.
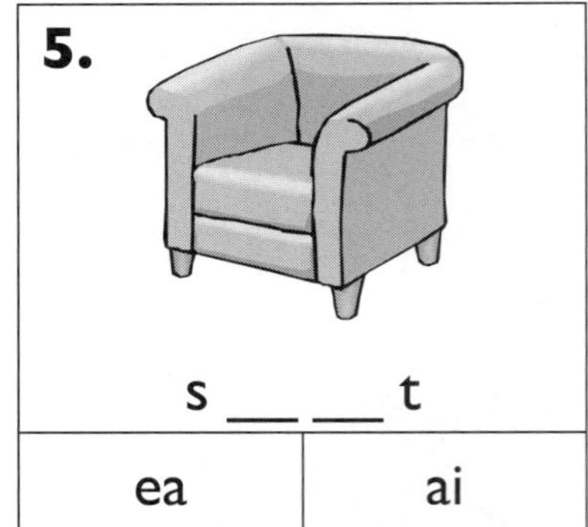

s ___ ___ t

ea	ai

6.

l ___ ___ n

io	ai

7.
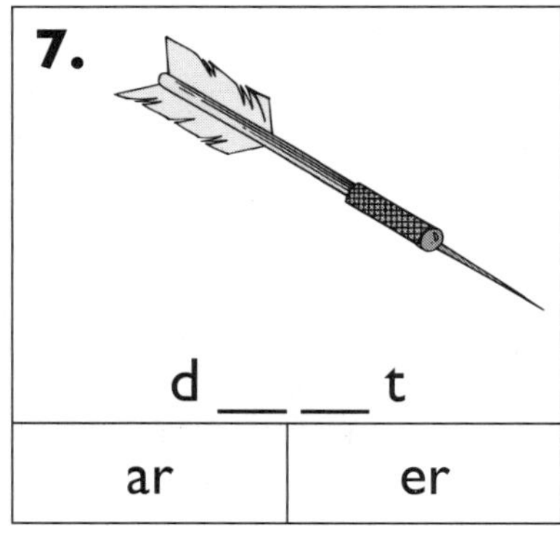

d ___ ___ t

ar	er

8.
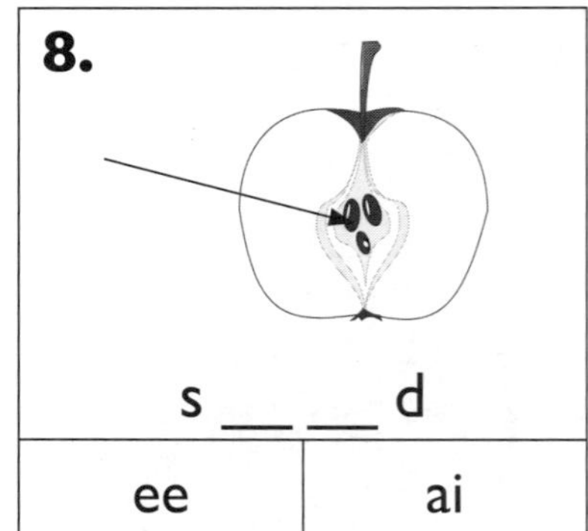

s ___ ___ d

ee	ai

9.
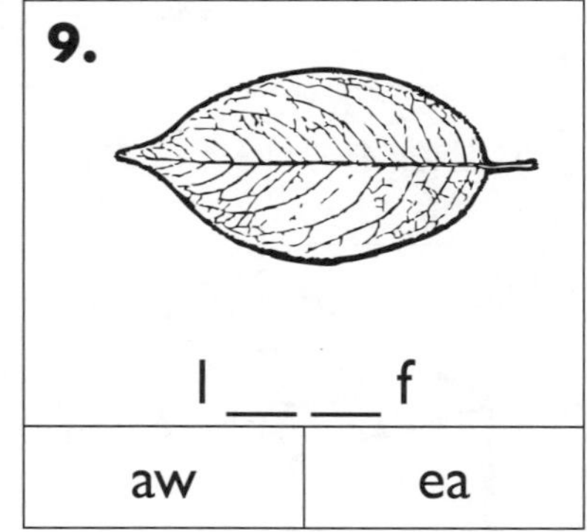

l ___ ___ f

aw	ea

10.
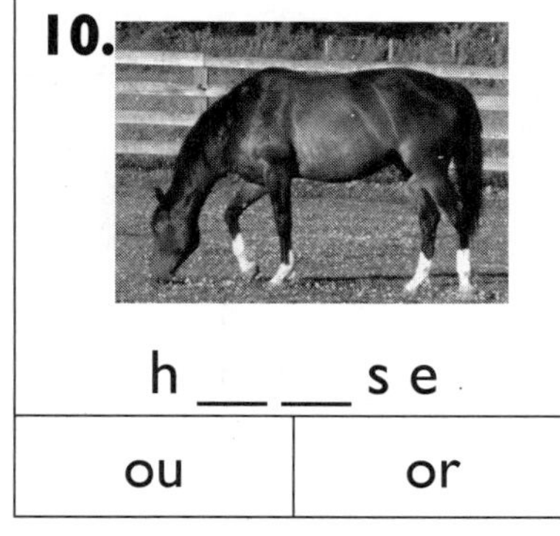

h ___ ___ s e

ou	or

11.
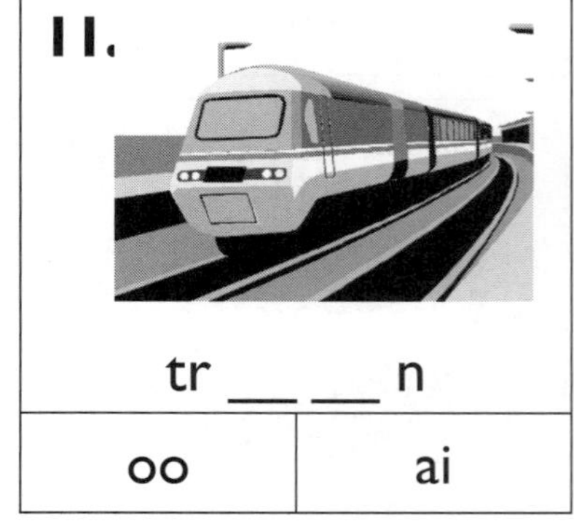

tr ___ ___ n

oo	ai

12.

cl ___ ___ n

or	ow

Matching Words and Pictures

Look at each picture. Say its name. Choose the right word for each picture and colour its box yellow.

1. 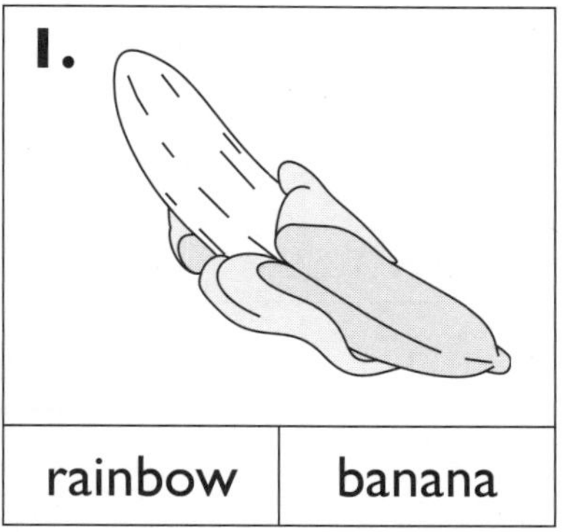

rainbow	banana

2. 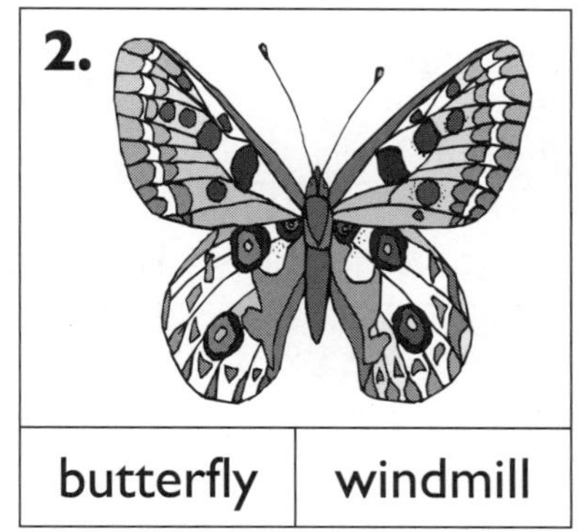

butterfly	windmill

3. 

clouds	bottle

4. 

mountain	dinosaur

5. 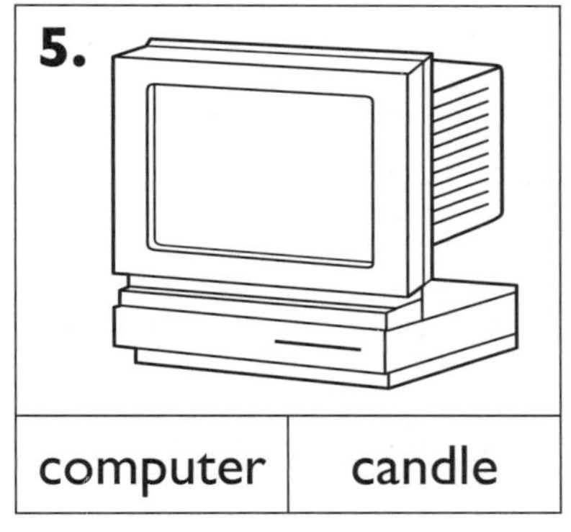

computer	candle

6. 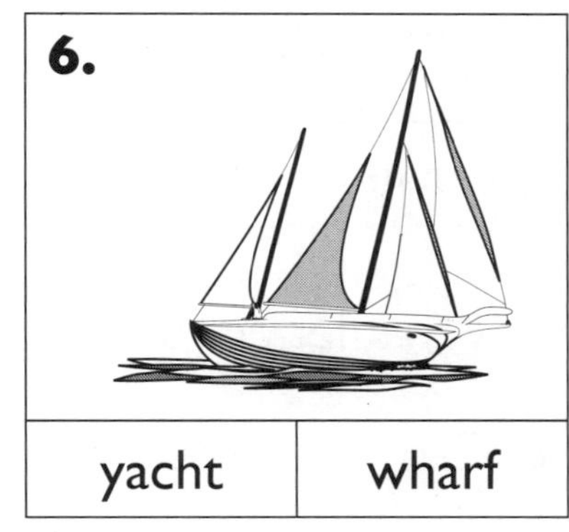

yacht	wharf

7. 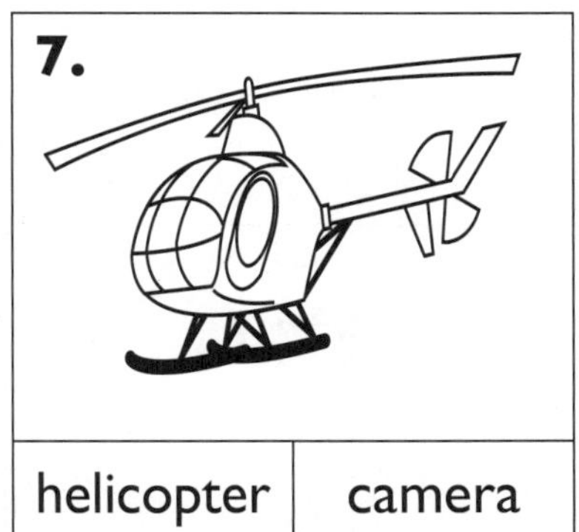

helicopter	camera

8. 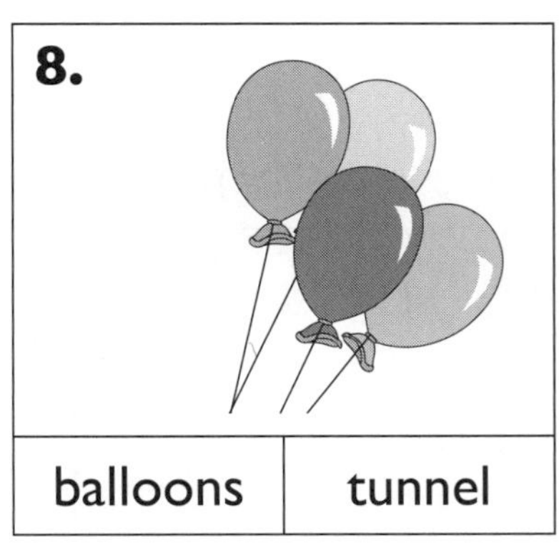

balloons	tunnel

9. 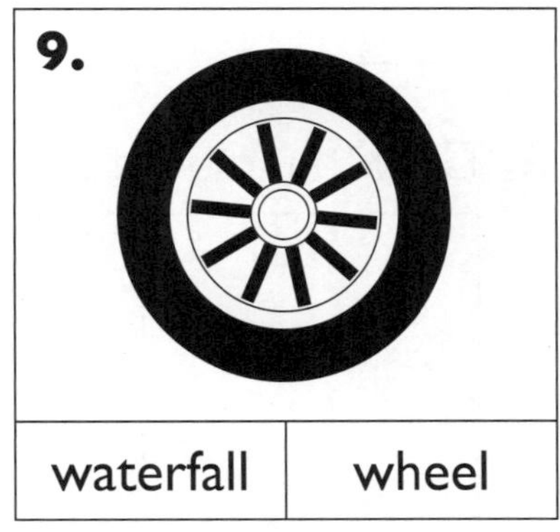

waterfall	wheel

10. 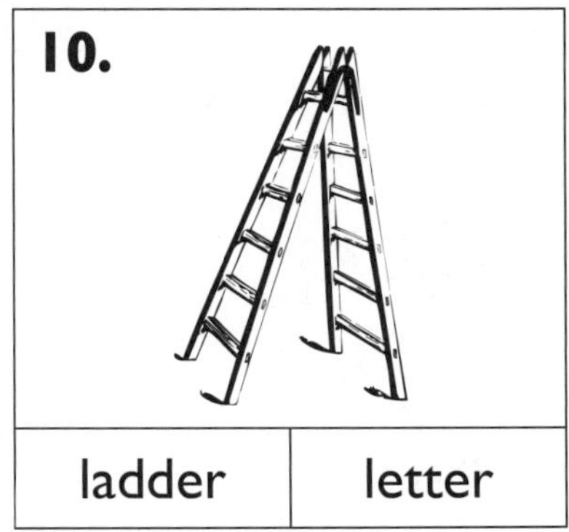

ladder	letter

11. 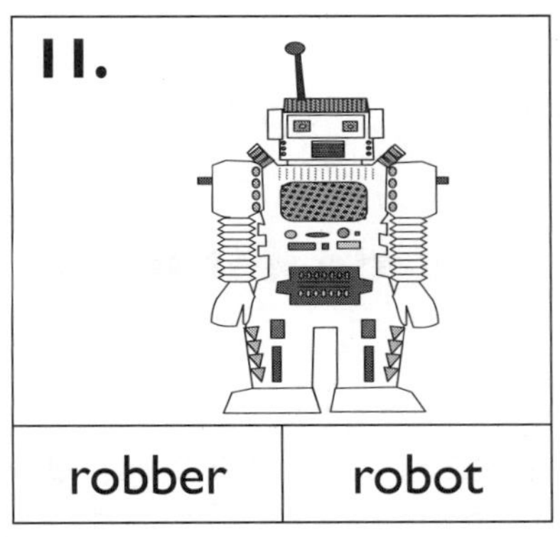

robber	robot

12. 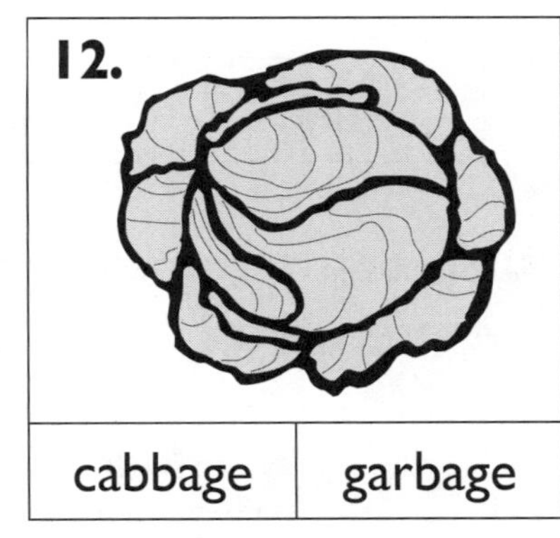

cabbage	garbage

Rhyming Words

Rhyming words end with the same sound. We all use rhyming words at one time or another. Sometimes we use them in games. We use them in songs, poems and ads on television. Some books even have titles that rhyme.

Have you read: ***Unreal, Banana Peel?*** __________

Do you say: ***See you later, alligator?*** __________

1. Some words that rhyme end with the same letters. The words

cat	bat	hat	sat	rat	mat	pat

all end with *at*.

Look at these words.

map	lap	tap	sap	rap

What letters do they all end with? __________

2. Can you write one more word that rhymes with these letters?

____

3. Draw a picture to match these rhyming words.

hen	pen	men	ten	Ben

4. Sometimes, words that rhyme **do not look the same**. Can you read these words?

four	sure	core	law	boar

Here is a poem about mice. All the rhyming words have been left out.

1. Read the poem once. Choose words from the box to fill the spaces. Remember: the word you choose must rhyme with the last word in the line above.

Mice

I think mice
Are rather ________ .
Their tails are long, their faces small,
They haven't any chins at __________ .
Their ears are pink, their teeth are white,
They run about the house at __________.
They nibble things they shouldn't touch,
And no one seems to like them __________.

But . . .

I think mice are nice!

Rose Fyleman

Use these words: all much nice night

2. All the words in each list rhyme — except one! Draw a circle around the word that does **NOT** rhyme with the other words in the list.

A	B	C
won	pour	rhyme
fun	core	time
bun	claw	slime
burn	floor	groom
son	blue	crime

Compound Words

Compound words are words made from two smaller words. The word *classroom* is made from the words *class* and *room*. Here are some more compound words. Can you read them?

backyard	rainbow	railway	today	cupboard	yourself	understand

1. Draw a picture for each of these compound words.

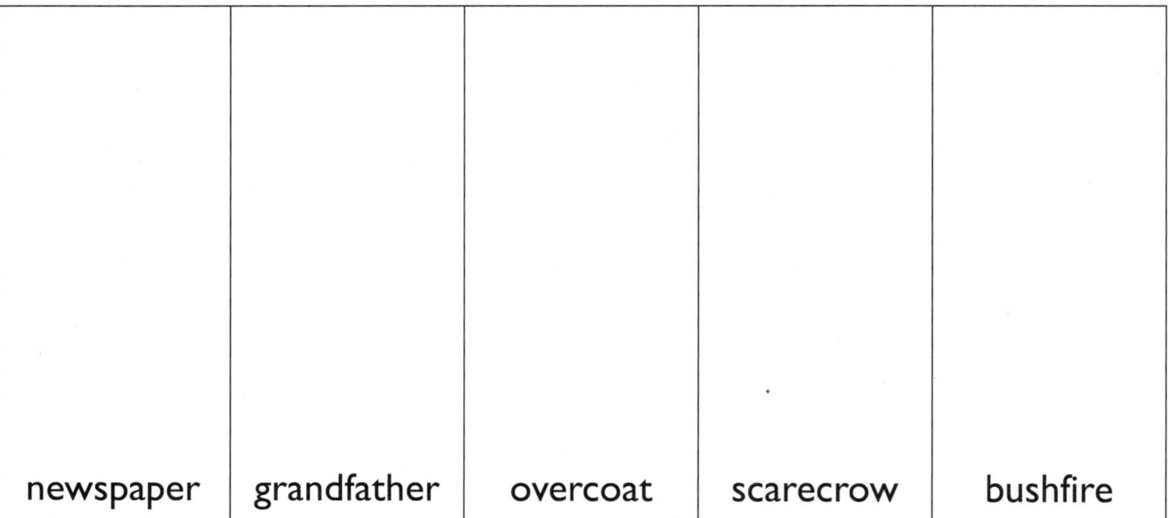

2. In each list, draw a line to join two small words that make one compound word.

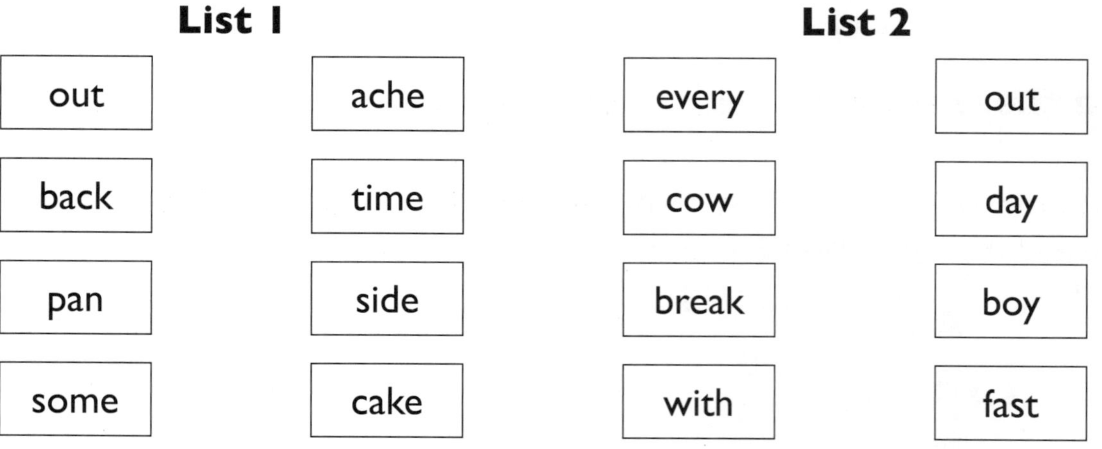

3. Use a compound word to describe these people:

a person who fights fires

a man who delivers letters

Recognising Silent Letters

Silent letters are a minor feature of the English language but it is important that students recognise them. One of the best ways to recognise silent letters is to experience a wide range of reading/spelling/editing activities. From such activities students will be alerted to the possibility of silent letters and will start to make the necessary generalisations.

1. Read these words. They all start with silent letters.

knee **gnat** **hour** **gnome** **knife**

Now circle the silent letters.

2. Read these words. There is a silent letter in each word.

calm **answer** **honest** **when** **scent**

Now circle the silent letters.

3. Read this short passage and circle all the words that have silent letters.

> When the whistle went we had finished the science lesson. Ms Knight said we should write a report. I wrote two pages — if you count the pictures!

4. Read these words. They are harder than the words above.

island **doubt** **rustle** **column** **plumber**

Now circle the silent letters.

5. Write the names of these pictures. Circle the silent letters.

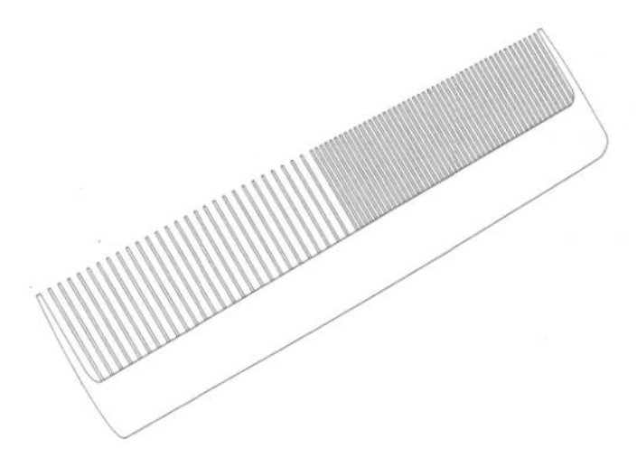

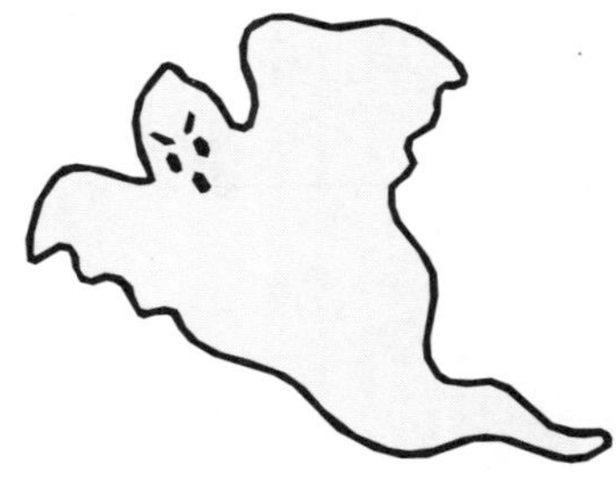

Following Instructions

This is an old nonsense verse. Read it to yourself and then read it aloud.

As I was going up the stairs
I met a man who wasn't there.
He wasn't there again today —
Oh, I wish he'd go away!

Anon.

Can you complete this picture by following the instructions?

1. There is a cupboard under the stairs. Colour the cupboard door green.
2. Put a handle on the door.
3. Number the steps. The first one is done for you.
4. The bottom step is shaded. Draw a teddy on the third step up.
5. Draw yourself sitting on the top step.
6. Write your name near your picture.
7. Draw a shoe on the step that is half-way up.
8. Colour the shoe brown.
9. Draw a ball bouncing down the stairs.

1

Name one thing you think could be in the cupboard under the stairs.

____

Understanding Questions

In comprehension exercises students will be given different types of questions. They are used to see just how well the student reads and how well they understand what they have read. A number of different types of questions are used in this book. For example:

- true or false (yes or no) questions
- short-answer questions
- matching exercises
- sequencing questions
- cloze exercises (filling in blanks)
- language-based questions
- multiple-choice questions
- full-sentence answer questions
- sentence-completing exercises
- labelling exercises
- open-ended questions (students might have to give their reasons)

Questions that want students to find information may begin with *How*, *When*, *Where* or *What*.

Questions that want students to give a reason will often begin with *Why*.

Some questions may ask students to give an opinion. For these, students have to express their own ideas.

Read this extract from 'Ideas About Space' by Colin Walker and answer the questions.

> People have always wondered about the things they see in the sky. They would see things and try to explain what they were.
>
> Some people thought the sun fell into the sea every night and came up the next morning.
>
> Lots of people thought the Earth was flat. They thought you could fall off the edge if you were careless.
>
> The Egyptians worshipped the sun and thought it sailed across the sky in a boat.
>
> Other people thought the sky was a big umbrella stretched over the Earth.

1. Who used to worship the sun? (full sentence answer)

The ____ .

2. Draw a line to match these sentence beginnings with their right endings.

Other people thought the sky was	**fell into the sea every night.**
People have always wondered about	**a big umbrella.**
Some people thought the sun	**the things they see in the sky.**

3. True or false? The Earth is flat. ☐ True ☐ False (Tick one box.)

Read some more from 'Ideas About Space' and answer the questions.

> As people learned more about the sky they changed their ideas.
> They found out that eclipses and comets did not mean that something bad was about to happen.
> They found out that the Earth was not really flat but round.
> They discovered that the Earth spins and orbits around the sun.
> As time went, on the telescope was invented. With telescopes people could learn more about space.
> New discoveries continue to change our ideas.
> Who knows what we will find out in years to come?

Write short answers (one or two words) to these questions.

1. What shape is the Earth? ____________________

2. What did people think comets could mean? ____________________

3. What invention helped people understand the sky? ____________________

4. Draw a line to match these sentence beginnings with the right endings.

The Earth spins	**they learned more about the sky.**
People changed their ideas as	**around the sun.**
People would see an eclipse	**in the sky.**

5. Label these pictures.

____

____

____

Read the passage from *Danny Dolphin's Holiday* by Gordon Winch and Gregory Blaxell. Answer the questions. Circle the correct letter for each one.

Danny Dolphin went on a holiday. He went to the Barrier Reef.

He saw the coral.
He saw the fish.
He saw the giant clams.
He saw the starfish.
He saw the sea horses.
He met a blue groper.
He met a white whale.
He met an octopus.
He met a reef shark and . . . he met Debbie Dolphin.

1. Danny Dolphin went to the Barrier Reef

(A) to go fishing. (B) for a holiday.
(C) to lie on the beach. (D) to ride sea horses.

2. When Danny went to the Great Barrier Reef he met

(A) a starfish. (B) sea horses.
(C) a dolphin. (D) giant clams.

3. Which creature do you think Danny Dolphin was most happy to meet? (There is a clue in the picture.)

(A) an octopus (B) a white whale
(C) a blue groper (D) Debbie Dolphin

4. Write the numbers 1, 2, 3, and 4 under the words to show the order in which Danny saw things on the Barrier Reef.

giant clams	coral	starfish	fish
________	________	________	________

In cloze exercises students select the best words to fill (close) the spaces. To do cloze exercises well, students should first read the title of the extract if there is one, then read the whole extract and look at any illustrations. When they have completed the exercise they should read it through again, from the beginning, to make sure it makes sense.

Read these extracts and choose the best word for each space from the list below. (Circle the correct letter — don't write in the space.)

On Saturday, there is a fete at our school. Our class is in charge of the Lucky Dip. We ____**1.**____ charge fifty cents a go. Everyone will win a prize.
Some of the prizes are little plastic toys. They were given to the ____**2.**____ for the fete. But we do have some really good prizes too. When my little brother has a go he hopes to ____**3.**____ ten free rides on the merry-go-round.

1. (A) will
(B) was
(C) had
(D) have

2. (A) crowd
(B) parents
(C) school
(D) visitors

3. (A) watch
(B) find
(C) buy
(D) win

One day dad brought home a big white goose. He asked me to look after it. It had belonged ____**4.**____ a man who worked on the same farm as my dad.

The goose was big. It was ____**5.**____ than a duck but smaller than a turkey. It ate grass faster than any sheep or goat. After a week, it had completely ____**6.**____ our back lawn!

4. (A) at
(B) to
(C) for
(D) with

5. (A) older
(B) faster
(C) better
(D) larger

6. (A) dug
(B) trimmed
(C) eaten
(D) cleaned

Finding Facts

When finding facts students will often be asked questions beginning with *Who*, *When*, *Where*, *What* and sometimes *How* and *Why*. Students may be asked to search for answers to questions that help them to understand the **time** and **place** of the action in an extract, as well as **who** is involved.

Most exercises in this part of the book are based upon **factual** writing. The extract below, Erosion on Earth, is a good place to start 'finding facts'. Students should answer with full-sentence answers unless told to do otherwise. Full-sentence answers help students to understand the questions and think through their answers.

Read this passage.

Erosion on Earth

by Colin Walker

Most things change as they get older.
Plants and animals change as they get older.
We change as we get older too.
The earth also changes. It erodes and wears away.
When big waves and storms crash against the land, parts of the land are worn away. This is called erosion.
Rivers cause erosion. When a river floods, soil, rocks and stones get swept away. They are sometimes swept out to sea.
When rain falls on bare ground, the earth can be eroded or worn away.
Dust storms can cause erosion.
Sharp dust can wear away the surface of very hard rocks.

1. What do most things do as they get older? (Complete the sentence.)

As things get older they ________________.

2. Where do rivers sometimes leave soil and rocks after a flood?

Rivers sometimes ________________________________

____.

3. When do plants change?

Plants change ________________________________.

4. Big waves cause erosion when they crash against the shore.

☐ True ☐ False (Tick one box.)

Sandra was given this note by her class teacher, Ms Brown, at the Sandbar Beach Public School. She was told to give it to her parents.

Circle the correct answer.

1. The water safety skills will be taught
   (A) at Sandbar Beach Public School.
   (B) in Sandbar Beach Sea Pool.
   (C) in Ms Brown's classroom.
   (D) on Ocean Road.

Water Safety Week

Next Week
Monday 4 January – Saturday 9 January

What do I bring?

¤ Clothes to swim in
¤ Plastic bag
¤ – and a towel!

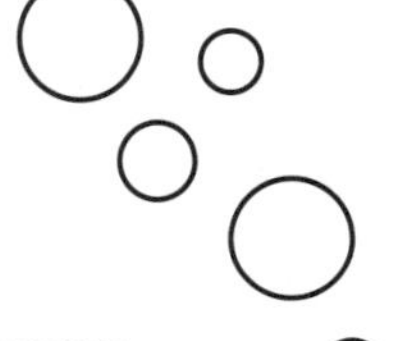

This is a great time for your child to learn safety skills with trained swimming teachers. Parking available in Ocean Road — just 5 minutes walk to the pool.

2. How many days will Water Safety Week go for? ________ days

3. Where can parents park their cars if they take their children to learn water safety skills?

   Parents ____

   ____.

4. Write the word that tells you that the swimming teachers know what they are doing. ________________

5. Water Safety skills will NOT be taught on
   (A) Monday. (B) Wednesday. (C) Saturday. (D) Sunday.

Read this passage from 'Weather on Earth' by Colin Walker and answer the questions.

Weather on Earth

by Colin Walker

Wherever we live on earth we get different kinds of weather.
It may rain in autumn and snow in winter.
It may be windy in spring and hot in summer.
The Earth's climate is different from season to season.
We have seasons because the Earth is tilted as it moves around the sun.

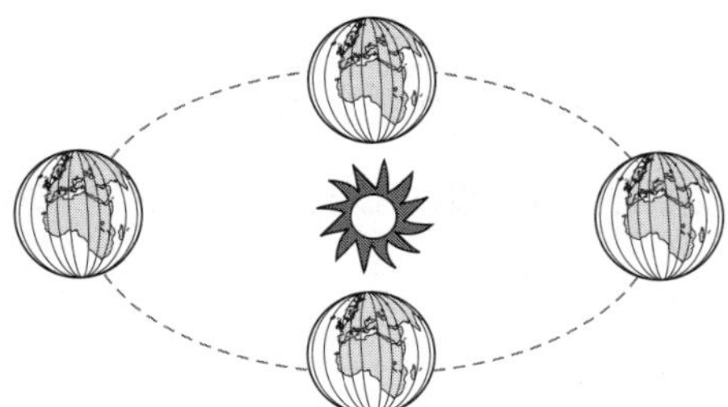

The part of the Earth that is tilted towards the sun is warm.
The part tilted away from the sun is cooler.
We can tell what our weather will be like most of the time.

1. Why do we have seasons?

We have seasons because ______________________________

____.

2. What part of the Earth is the warmest?

____.

3. Draw a line to match the season with the weather.

Summer	sunny
Autumn	cold
Winter	windy
Spring	hot

Poisonous Creatures

Do snakes make your skin crawl? Do they give you nightmares? Whether you love them or hate them, everyone finds snakes and spiders fascinating. People go to zoos and places like the Australian Reptile Park to get a closer, and sometimes shivery, look.

Most Australian spiders are harmless but some are really dangerous. One of the most dangerous spiders lives in Australia's largest city — Sydney. It is the Sydney funnel-web. The male funnel-web is smaller than the female but he is much more deadly. He is one of the world's most deadly spiders.

The Australian Reptile Park keeps funnel-webs. People visit the park to see the spiders. People at the park collect their **poison** (venom). The spiders are 'milked' and the poison is used to make a treatment for people who have been bitten.

1. Where do many funnel-web spiders live? ______________________________

____.

2. The female funnel-web spider is larger than the male.

☐ True ☐ False

3. People go to the Australian Reptile Park to see spiders and ____________ .

4. A person who is bitten by a funnel-web will certainly die.

☐ True ☐ False

5. What word could be used instead of *poison*? ____________________ (one word)

6. The Australian Reptile Park keeps spiders to

(A) scare people.

(B) collect their poison.

(C) give people nightmares.

(D) protect people from being bitten.

Understanding Narratives

Simply put, narrative texts tell a story. They can entertain or instruct, or do both; just consider Aesop's fables. At the Year 1–2 level, narratives generally involve a series of events in chronological order. Narratives can include historical recounts, fables, myths, legends, comics, verse, plays, and fairy tales.

The Old Ship

by Gordon Winch and Gregory Blaxell

One day Danny Dolphin found a ship. The ship was very old.
He found an anchor on the ship. The anchor was very old.
He found a mast on the ship. The mast was very old.
He found a cannon on the ship. The cannon was very old.
He found a bell on the ship. The bell was very old.
He found a bottle on the ship. The bottle was very old.
He found a cabin on the ship. The cabin was very old.
Inside the old cabin he found an old box. Inside the old box he found . . . treasure.

1. Where do you think Danny Dolphin found the old ship? ______________

____

2. Draw a line from the things Danny found to show the order in which he found them.

anchor	treasure	ship
first	second	last

3. Draw a picture of Danny and the old ship. Put these on your ship and label each one.

an anchor

a mast

a cannon

a bell

The Lion and the Mouse

by Aesop

A mouse was running through the forest when it tripped over the paw of a lion. Waking up, the lion grabbed the mouse then raised the small mouse to its mouth.

The mouse was terrified. "Please don't eat me," it begged. "One day I will repay you, if you spare my life."

This made the lion laugh and he let the mouse go.

The lion soon forgot the little mouse. He never thought he would see it again. But later, the lion was caught in a net by some hunters. They wanted to sell the lion to a circus. They made sure the lion could not escape from their net while they went to get help.

The lion roared in anger. He struggled against the tight ropes.

The mouse heard the roars, and running to the spot saw the trapped lion. It gnawed through the ropes before the hunters returned.

"You laughed at me, the other day," said the little mouse, when they were safely away, "and you did not expect me to repay your kindness. Now you can see that even a little mouse can help a mighty lion."

1. What do you think would be another good title for this story?

(A) The Circus (B) The Good Deed

(C) The Greedy Lion (D) The Small Mouse

2. Draw four pictures to show the order in which things happened in the story.

1.	2.	3.	4.

3. The hunters wanted to sell the lion to ______________________________ .

4. The lion expected the little mouse would help him. ☐ True ☐ False

Where's my Ticket?

by Helen Andersen and Bill Reinholdt

Penny was driven to Temby Primary School by her Mum every day. They always went the same way.

Penny always enjoyed the drive to school, because it was the only time in all the day when she and her Mum got to talk without her big sister Sally being there.

They always left at half-past eight and usually arrived at a quarter to nine. The school had a garden, a climbing frame and lots of good climbing trees. Penny liked getting there early to play before school started.

Today was different. Although it was the holidays, Mum and Penny were going to school by train. Well, they were not really going to school, but they were practising how to get there! Penny's mother was starting a new job next term and Penny would have to take the train to school, all on her own.

1. Penny had always gone to school with her mother. ☐ True ☐ False

2. Penny was older than Sally. ☐ True ☐ False

3. How do you think Penny would feel on the first day of school in the new term? ______________. Do you have a reason? (No written answer is required.)

4. Penny liked going to school with her mother because she

(A) always went the same way.

(B) did not like going on the train.

(C) enjoyed going to school with Sally.

(D) could talk to her mother without anyone else being there.

5. Penny could do many things before school started. Penny did NOT do one of these. Which one?

(A) climb trees

(B) play in the garden

(C) finish her homework

(D) play on the climbing frame

Thunk the Dinosaur's Big Surprise

by Lisby Gore

It was that time of the year when the sun was high in the sky, the days were warm and it was light until after bedtime. It was also only two days until Thunk's birthday.

Thunk, the Tyrannosaurus Rex, was sitting at the opening of his cave when Three Prongs, the Dryosuarus, bounded up.

"Guess what, guess what?" said Three Prongs.

"I know," replied Thunk, "it's nearly my birthday!"

"No, not that," Three Prongs moaned, having heard all about Thunk's birthday for weeks. "Dennis has found a great slide. It starts at Curly Rocks and goes down to Lake Murky. It's so much fun, you've got to come."

They reached Curly Rocks but Dennis, the Stegosaurus, was nowhere to be seen.

"The best way to slide is by sitting on a large palm leaf," said Three Prongs.

They both picked out a large palm leaf. "You go first," said Three Prong.

Thunk sat down on his leaf, moved himself to the top of the path and set off yelling, "Last one to the bottom is a smelly egg!"

1. Do you think this is a true story? ☐ Yes ☐ No

2. Three Prongs went to see Thunk
   (A) to get a large palm leaf.
   (B) to wish him "Happy birthday".
   (C) to take him to a new slide he had found.
   (D) because he was worried about Dennis.

3. What was Thunk thinking about when Three Prongs came to see him?
   (Tick one box.) ☐ his birthday ☐ Dennis ☐ playing on the new slide

4. From the story find: a compound word ____________________

a word that ends with *th* ____________________

Understanding Conversations

In Year 1 and 2, most students need to know how to interpret a wide variety of speech 'signs' when reading.

Speech marks, or quotation marks, are written as double marks (" "). They are used in **direct speech**. Example: "Who's at the door?" she asked.

Each time there is a change of speaker there is a new paragraph.

The Park Street Playground

by Joy Cowley

The playground in Park Street was old and broken. It wasn't safe to play in. So the very wise children of Park Street went to see the mayor about a new place to play.

"That playground is a junk yard!" the very wise children said to the mayor. "It's a mess! It's utterly gross! Please, Mr Mayor, will you give us a new playground?"

"I'd like to help you," said the Mayor, "but the city doesn't have the money or the space for a new playground. Tell you what! I'll make a deal with you. I'll give you everything you need to fix the playground, if you get your parents to do all the work."

The very wise children thought that was a good idea. But their mums and dads already worked. When would the playground get done?

"What about early Saturday morning?" said the Mayor. And so it was a deal.

But as every wise child knows parents don't like getting up early on Saturday mornings. The wise children had to work out a plan for getting mums and dads out of bed.

1. This passage is a conversation between some children and the ________.

2. Add the speech marks to this sentence.

☐ That playground is a junk yard! ☐ said the children.

3. Colour the boxes to show the things you would find in a park.

☐ swings	☐ shopping centre	☐ see-saw
☐ rainbow	☐ climbing frame	☐ television
☐ slippery dip	☐ panda	☐ picnic tables

The Meeting

"Why can't I come with you?" asked Annie as her aunt got ready to leave.

Aunty kissed her on the cheek. "Because you're only nine and children aren't supposed to go to meetings."

Annie said, "I won't make a noise."

"I'm sure you won't," agreed her aunty, "but it will be a long meeting and not very interesting for children."

Annie couldn't think why a meeting about having a street fair in her street would not be interesting.

"Why not?" asked Annie. "I love street fairs."

"We'll only be talking about what to do," explained her aunty. "We won't be *having* a street fair."

"Oh," murmured Annie, a little surprised.

1. Writers often use the word *said* to show when people speak. What other words are used instead of *said* in this story? (Find three words.)

________________, ________________, ________________

2. How many people are having a conversation in *The Meeting*? __________

3. Why do you think Annie was a little surprised? (A full-sentence answer is required.)

____

____

4. Add the speech marks to this sentence.

☐ What did you think I was going to do? ☐ asked Annie's aunty.

5. Complete this sentence. Do not use the word *said.*

"Everyone out of the pool!" ________________ the swimming coach.

6. Write your own speech sentence here.
(Some of the things you might have to use are: capital letters, speech marks, full stops, commas.)

____

____

The Playground

The Mayor marched up to the park. He had heard some really strange things.

"This is ridiculous!" he declared.

"No it isn't!" said Thomas, as he slid down the slide and landed at the Mayor's feet.

"This playground is dangerous," announced the Mayor.

"**No, it isn't! It isn't!**"

The Mayor repeated himself. "This playground is dangerous!"

Other children came over to see why the Mayor was raising his voice.

"No, it is not!" said Kevin, standing as tall as he possibly could.

The Mayor looked down at him. "Excuse me, but who are you?" asked the Mayor.

"Kevin. And I helped fix up the park to make it safe!" said Kevin.

"Kevin and his dad painted the see-saw," said Thomas.

"My dad owns the hardware shop," added Kevin, quite proudly.

"Oh my, oh my," mumbled the Mayor to himself. He found small children difficult to talk to. He would much rather be giving speeches in the Town Hall or declaring school fetes open.

1. How many people spoke during the conversation? ________________

2. Who said, "No, it isn't! It isn't!" in the passage? ________________

3. Add the speech marks to this sentence.

The Mayor asked, ☐ Who else helped in the playground? ☐

4. Write three words that are used instead of *said*.

__________________, __________________, __________________

5. Circle the correct word in the brackets to complete the sentence.

(**Kevin's** **Thomas's**) father owns a hardware shop.

Sequencing Skills

Sequencing refers to the order things are done in or the order in which they happen. Instructions are given in a sequence which we are meant to follow. Instructions are used in recipes, training programs, exams and magic tricks.

In most stories we read of events that follow one after another. Diaries are a good example of events happening in a time sequence, but even simple nursery rhymes may tell a story in sequence.

Sometimes authors will present the sequence of events 'out of order' to make their stories interesting and mysterious.

In sequencing events students should understand such terms as *before, after, then, during, later* and *earlier* as well as *first, second* . . . and so on to *last*. In some sequencing exercises students are asked to put sentences or events in order.

Read this short poem.

Solomon Grundy

Solomon Grundy,
Born on Monday,
Named on Tuesday,
Married on Wednesday,
Took sick on Thursday,
Worse on Friday,
Dead on Saturday,
Buried on Sunday,
And that was the end of Solomon Grundy.

1. What happened to Solomon Grundy before he was named?

Before he was named Solomon Grundy was _______________ .

2. When did Solomon Grundy get sick? On _______________.

3. What happened after Solomon Grundy died?

After Solomon Grundy died he _______________________________ .

4. Which event happened first? (A) Solomon Grundy got married.

(B) Solomon Grundy got sick.

5. Do you think Solomon Grundy really did all these things in one week?

____

Page 3 — Using Basic Sight Words

1.–4. Parent/teacher to check. 5. children, drink, house, school, baby

Revision of Reading Skills

Alphabetical Order

Page 4

1.

A	B	C	D	E	F	G
H	I	J	K	L	M	N
O	P	Q	R	S	T	U
V	W	X	Y	Z		

2. Parent/teacher to check 3. a whale

Page 5

1. aunty, bike, elephant,

2.

A		B		C	
4	robot	5	window	4	sand
1	astronaut	1	door	2	castle
3	orbit	3	rug	5	wave
5	space	2	kitchen	3	fish
2	moon	4	television	1	bucket

3. bottle, flag, house, rabbit, weather, then any word that starts with x, y or z.

Page 6 — Recognising Initial Sounds

1. b 2. j 3. t 4. f 5. m 6. v 7. g 8. r 9. z 10. dr 11. cl 12. th 13. sn 14. gr 15. fr

Page 7 — Recognising Final Sounds

1. b 2. l 3. s 4. d 5. n 6. x 7. g 8. p 9. d 10. ck 11. sh 12. ng 13. th 14. st 15. lt

Page 8 — Spelling with Blends

1. fork 2. rain 3. bear, 4. moon 5. seat 6. lion 7. dart 8. seed 9. leaf 10. horse 11. train 12. clown

Page 9 — Matching Words and Pictures

1. banana 2. butterfly 3. clouds 4. dinosaur 5. computer 6. yacht 7. helicopter 8. balloons 9. wheel 10. ladder 11. robot 12. cabbage

Rhyming Words

Page 10

1. ap 2. gap, nap, etc. 3. Parent/teacher to check 4. Parent/teacher to check

Page 11

1. nice, all, night, much 2. A. burn B. blue C. groom

Page 12

1. Parent/teacher to check
2. **List 1.** backache, outside, sometime, pancake
   List 2. everyday, cowboy, breakfast, without
3. firefighter, postman

Page 13 — Recognising Silent Letters

1. (k, g, h, g, k) 2. calm, answer, honest, when, scent. 3. When the whistle went we had finished the science lesson. Ms Knight said we should write a report. I wrote two pages — if you count the pictures! 4. (s, b, t, n, b)
5. comb, palm, ghost

Page 14 — Following Instructions
Parent or teacher to check.

Understanding Questions

Page 15
1. The Egyptians used to worship the sun. 2. Other people thought the sky was a big umbrella. People have always wondered about/the things they see in the sky. Some people thought the sun/fell into the sea every night. 3. False

Page 16
1. round 2. something bad was about to happen 3. telescope 4. The earth spins / around the sun. People changed their ideas as / they learned more about the sky. People would see an eclipse / in the sky. (**Note:** You shouldn't look an eclipse. It could damage your eyes.) 5. Earth, telescope, comet

Page 17
1. (B) 2. (C) 3. (D) 4. Sequencing (3, 1, 4, 2)

Page 18
1. (A) 2. (C) 3. (D) 4. (B) 5. (D) 6. (C)

Finding Facts

Page 19 (Answers may vary.)
1. As things get older they **change**. 2. Rivers sometimes **leave (put) soil and rocks in the sea**.
3. Plants change **as they get older.** 4. True

Page 20
1. (B) 2. 6 days 3. Parents can park their cars in Ocean Road 4. trained 5. (D)

Page 21
1. the Earth is tilted (as it moves around the sun) 2. The part of the Earth that is tilted towards the sun is warmest. 3 Summer/hot, Autumn/windy, Winter/cold, Spring/sunny

Page 22
1. Many funnel-web spiders live in Sydney. 2. True 3. snakes 4. False
5. venom 6. (B)

Understanding Narratives

Page 23
1. (I think) Danny Dolphin found the old ship under the sea. 2. anchor/second, treasure/last, ship/first
3. Parent or teacher to check

Page 24
1. (B) The Good Deed 2. Parent/teacher to check 3. a circus 4. False

Page 25
1. True 2. False 3. Answers will vary. (scared) 4. (D) 5. (C)

Page 26
1. No 2. (C) 3 his birthday. 4. himself/birthday/bedtime/nowhere, both/path

Understanding Conversations

Page 27
1. Mayor 2. "That playground is a junk yard!" said the children. 3. swings, slippery dip, climbing frame, see-saw, picnic tables

Page 28
1. asked, agreed, explained, murmured 2. two 3. Answers will vary. 4. "What did you think I was going to do?" asked Annie's aunty. 5. called, shouted, warned, etc. 6. Parent/teacher to mark.

Page 29
1. three 2. Thomas 3. The Mayor asked, "Who else helped in the playground?" 4. declared, added, announced, asked, mumbled 5. Kevin's

Sequencing Skills

Page 30
1. born 2. On Thursday 3. was buried 4. (A) 5. No

Page 31
1. Parent/teacher to check. 2. False 3. before 4. tooting (their horns) 5. Answers will vary.

Page 32
1. (2, 1, 3, 4) 2. (3, 2, 1) 3. (C)

Page 33
1. (2, 1, 3) 2. (1, 4, 3, 2) 3. catch (some) numbats; study numbats/keep notes; free

Page 34
1. put (a thick layer of) newspaper on your table. 2. (C) 3. True 4. scratch line pictures in the melted crayon

Following Directions

Page 35
1. 6 steps 2. These instructions help you make a telephone call (from home). 3. After you have hung up, you are reminded to thank your parents for letting you use the phone. 4. the person answering the call 5. the numbers in (correct) order. 6. hang up (replace the receiver)

Page 36
1. three 2. five 3. to tie around the neck of the balloon (to stop the air from coming out) 4. Parent/teacher to check 5. Last 6. First

Page 37
1. Drain the juice from the pineapple pieces. 2. two 3. grated cheese 4. (2, 1, 4, 3) 5. True 6. (D)

Page 38
1. six 2. horns, arms, legs or feelers 3. glued 4. a parent 5. Parent/teacher to check.

Page 39
1. bucket, spade, (plastic) knife 2. make the building surface as flat as possible 3. damp 4. moat, castle, shells 5. Parent/teacher to check

Understanding Descriptions

Page 40
1. clock 2. bottle 3. table 4. skateboard

Page 41
1. legs/clothes pegs; nose/ice-cream cone; mouth/dog's bone; head/square 2. Answers will vary — less than one metre 3. Parent/teacher to mark.

Page 42
1. tents 2. caves 3. food, water 4. Answers will vary: weather/wind/rain, etc. 5. and 6. Parent/teacher to check.

Page 43
1. clumsy 2. puffed, wheezed 3. (A) 4. The buttered toast landed / on Samson's mother's head. Samson had to ride / up a long hill. The juice went / all over the bed.

Understanding Explanations

Page 44
1. facts 2. True 3. (A) 4. Parent/teacher to check

Page 45
1. colours 2. Answers will vary. 3. Parent/teacher to check. 4. True

Answers

Extension Cloze Exercises

Page 46
years, were, deep, drinks, tombs, women

Page 47
1. (B) her, 2. (B) with, 3. (A) found, 4. (C) looked, 5. (A) All, 6. (C) left 7. (A) are, (B) shouted/ roared/etc, (C) very, (D) counted/sorted

Pages 48–49
1.(A) sell 2. (C) along 3. (D) money 4. (A) richer 5. But 6. hot 7. feeds 8. easily 9. thunder, fell, ugly, sharp, shark, saw, move 10. bed, day, autumn, where

Reading Poetry

Page 50
1. socks, one 2. reach, teach, bleach, leech, etc. 3. sandwiches 4. hats 5. False 6. False 7. summer 8. Parent/teacher to check.

Page 51
1. rivers, trees, cattle 2. (B) 3. air/sky, garden, roof 4. countryside 5. List 1: wide, down, List 2: blue, swing

Page 52
1. (In case) a fairy (comes along.) 2. (B) 3. think them out 4. fly away 5. Answers will vary. 6. Answers will vary.

Page 53
1. (D) 2. Parent/teacher to check. 3. Answers will vary. 4. spade/made, wave/brave, aside/tide

Appreciating Fables, Legends and Traditional Stories

Page 54
1. (B) 2. (C) 3. Answers will vary. 4. True 5. numbat, goanna.

Page 55
1. False 2. sea 3. (D)

Page 56
1. bold 2. shrieking/squeaking 3. cats, hats, vats, sprats, chats, flats
4. Answers will vary. (scared) 5. Parent/teacher to check.

Reading Picture Narratives

Page 57
1. 4 2. (B) 3. very large 4. Parent/teacher to check

Page 58
1. Answers will vary — it's the things that you do and hear when your picture is being taken. 2. Loren 3. happy. 4. Parent/teacher to mark.

Interpreting Notices

Page 59
1. netball or T-ball 2. netball 3. yearly 4. Tuesday (25 November) 5. swimming (Learn to Swim)

Page 60
1. Terrier, Sam 2. Ring Pet Search. 3. Answers may vary. (All, except age.) 4. False 5. one year old

Robot Walk

Dad said, "If you're going to town, take the robot with you. It's getting rusty. It needs a walk."

"But it hasn't got any road sense," I complained.

"It'll be all right," said Dad.

So I took the robot for a walk. What a disaster!

The robot wanted to walk on the road. Cars were tooting at it.

"Walk on the footpath!" I told it. "That's what footpaths are for."

The robot walked on the footpath, but it walked too fast and bumped into people.

"That's not smart," I said. "You might hurt someone. Look where you are going!"

We wanted to cross the road. The robot walked out into the traffic. I grabbed it by the hand. "Stop! We have to cross at the crossing!"

We got to the crossing. The sign said: DON'T WALK. Can you guess what happened?

1. Draw pictures to show the order in which the robot did the wrong things.

walking on the road	**bumping into people**	**crossing the road**

2. While the robot was on the footpath there was no trouble. ____________

☐ True ☐ False

3. The robot didn't look at the sign (**before after while**) crossing the road.

4. During the robot's walk down the road cars were ____________________.

5. What do you think happened next? ____________________________

____

Here are three sequencing exercises. Students are asked to correctly sequence the pictures or statements.

1. Write the numbers in the boxes to show the correct order.

☐ ☐ ☐ ☐

2. Read these sentences about pandas and then use the numbers 1, 2 and 3 to show the correct order. When you have finished, read the sentences aloud to make sure they make sense.

☐ Today they are only found in six small areas in western China.

☐ Two thousand years ago, pandas were still common in China.

☐ Thousands of years ago, pandas lived in many parts of China.

3. Read this short passage.

> Danh got his towel and swimming bag and went to the pool.
> At the pool there was a big sign: SWIMMING CARNIVAL TODAY.
> He paid his money to go in.
> Danh changed into his swimming costume.
> Then he sat in the stand and waited for the call for his race.
> Finally they called his race. "Eight year old boys, freestyle, to the blocks now."

What do you think Danh did next?

(A) Danh decided to buy his lunch.

(B) Danh found a better place to watch the race.

(C) Danh went to the starting blocks.

(D) Danh jumped into the pool.

1. Use the numbers 1, 2 and 3 to show the correct order of these sentences. When you have finished, read the sentences aloud in order to make sure the story makes sense.

☐ "See who is at the door, dear," my mother said.

☐ Just then there was a knock on the front door.

☐ When I opened the door a lady stood outside smiling at me.

2. Use the numbers 1, 2, 3 and 4 to show the correct order of these sentences. When you have finished, read the sentences aloud in order to make sure the story makes sense.

☐ I listened to my parents who had been looking into my room.

☐ Dad replied, "I don't know if they would be big enough!"

☐ "Just like the ones you see in the street," agreed my mum.

☐ "First," said Dad, "we should ring for a big rubbish bin."

3. Tony is a park ranger. One of his jobs is to learn more about numbats.

Numbat Run! by Jill Morris

First Tony had to catch some numbats. Then he put special collars on them so that he could study where they went.

Tony had other people helping him study numbats. They filled dozens of notebooks with their notes.

Tony bred numbats in zoos. Some numbats were taken to the Perth Zoo. Later, both adults and babies were returned to the forest.

What is the first thing Tony had to do? He had to ______________________

____.

Other people helped Tony to ______________________________________.

After the numbats were bred in safety, they were set ____________________

____.

I like having surprises when I make pictures. That's why I like melted crayon pictures. You can make melted crayon pictures too. This is what you do.

Melted Crayon Picture

What you will need

- Bits of wax crayons. The bits you find in your pencil case can be used or you could ask an adult to shave bits off your good crayons.
- Two sheets of art paper or plain paper
- Several sheets of newspaper
- An iron (you should get the help of an adult)

What to do

Put a thick layer of newspaper on a table.
Put one sheet of art paper on top of the newspaper.
Spread bits of crayon all over the art paper.
Put the second sheet of art paper on top of the first.
Using a warm iron (you will need the help of an older person) press on the top sheet and melt the crayon bits and shavings.
Peel off the top sheet of paper and use your imagination to find colourful shapes of things you know, or you can scratch line pictures in the melted crayon using the point of a pair of scissors or a pointed stick.

1. Before you start making your picture you should ______________________

____.

2. The bits of wax crayons are spread
(A) over the newspaper.
(B) under the sheets of art paper.
(C) between the two sheets of art paper.

3. You do not know what your picture will look like until you take the top sheet of art paper off the bottom sheet. ☐ True ☐ False

4. What is the last thing you might do to complete your picture?
To complete the picture you can ______________________________.

Following Directions

When students want to know how to make something they have to follow a procedure or follow a set of directions. Each part of the directions (instructions) is called a step.

Printed material that tells how to do things can be found around the home, such as how to put a film in camera or how to bake a cake.

Students will find many books that give directions in their school library: how to play sport, how to do magic tricks, how to do experiments, how to recycle waste materials, and so on.

Some directions are simple, such as a sign on a railway station that tells the passengers how to get a ticket from a ticket machine.

Read the following set of simple instructions.

How to make a telephone call from a home phone *the aim*

You will need: a telephone, (and something to say!) *the materials*

The steps: 1. Lift the telephone receiver. *what you have to do*

2. Listen for the dial tone.
3. Dial the phone number. Press each number in order.
4. Wait for the person called to answer.
5. Have your conversation.
6. Replace the receiver (hang up). *final step*

Remember: thank your parents for the use of the phone.

1. How many steps are there in making a phone call from home? ____________

2. What does this set of instructions help you to do? (Complete the sentence.)

These ____

____.

3. What are you reminded to do after you have hung up? (A full-sentence answer is required.)

____.

4. Who is most likely to speak first in a telephone conversation? (Tick one box.)

☐ the person making the call ☐ the person answering the call

5. When you dial the phone number, be sure to press ____________

____.

6. What is the last step in making a telephone call? ____________

Even for the simplest things the instructions can seem hard!

How to Blow Up a Balloon

You will need

a balloon
a piece of string
a person to blow up the balloon

Steps

1. First pick up the balloon and put the opening in your mouth.
2. Hold the opening with your fingers so that when you blow the air goes in the balloon.
3. Next you have to blow hard until the balloon grows to the size you want.
4. When it is the right size, twist the tube at the top of the balloon around to stop the air escaping.
5. Last of all, tie the string around the opening to keep the air in.

Answer questions 1 to 3 with short answers.

1. How many 'things' do you need to blow up a balloon? ________________

2. How many steps are in the instructions to blow up a balloon? ________

3. What is the string used for? ______________________________________

____

4. Decorate the space inside the instruction box with balloons of different colours.

Use the words *first* and *last* to complete questions 5 and 6.

5. ______________ of all, tie the string around the opening to keep the air in.

6. ______________ you have to put the opening in your mouth.

Tropical Melts Recipe

Ingredients

4 crumpets
butter or margarine
4 slices of ham
small can of pineapple pieces
1 small cup grated cheese
Serves 2

Directions

Drain the juice from the pineapple pieces.
Toast crumpets until brown on both sides.
Spread butter on crumpets
Add one slice of ham to each crumpet.
Add a spoonful of pineapple pieces.
Cover with grated cheese.
Grill until cheese melts.
Serve immediately with salad.

1. After collecting the ingredients, what is the first step in making Tropical Melts? ____________________________________

2. This recipe makes enough Tropical Melts for __________ people.

3. What is the last ingredient to be added to the crumpet top? (Tick one box.)

☐ grated cheese ☐ sliced ham ☐ pineapple pieces

4. Number the boxes 1 to 4 to show the order for making Tropical Melts.

☐ Toast the crumpets.

☐ Drain the juice from the pineapple pieces.

☐ Grill the crumpets until cheese melts.

☐ Add the toppings to the crumpets.

5. If you don't have butter you can use margarine. ☐ True ☐ False

6. The words *serve immediately* instruct you to serve Tropical Melts
(A) when everyone is ready.
(B) when the crumpets are buttered.
(C) when the Melts have cooled down.
(D) as soon as the Melts have finished grilling.

Want to make something for your best friend? How about a little monster to watch him or her from the top of a pencil?

Let's Make . . . Pencil Top Monsters

You will need . . .

Some ping-pong balls Strong glue Pipe-cleaners Textas
Safety knife
Odd buttons or 'eyes' (You can buy fun 'eyes' at many craft stores.)

Instructions

1. Ask a parent to cut a hole in the ping-pong ball just big enough to push a pencil in.
2. Using the ping-pong ball as the head of your monster, draw a mouth, nose and eyes using texta colours, or you can glue on buttons to make eyes.
3. Use pipe cleaners to make horns, arms, legs or feelers. Make sure that they are glued on carefully. Glue beads onto the end of the pipe cleaners to make eyes on stalks. Buttons could be used to make feet.
4. Stick on buttons to decorate your monster with special features. Use your imagination freely.

Give the pencil to your friend.

Answer questions 1 and 2 with short answers.

1. How many 'things' do you need to make pencil top monsters?

2. Name one thing the pipe cleaners can be used for. ________________

3. The eyes can be drawn on or they can be ________________ on.

4. Who should use the safety knife? ________________

5. Draw a picture of a pencil top monster here.
Give your pencil top monster a name.

____

Building a Sandcastle

Many people love going to the beach. Some people like to play in the waves and others like to build sandcastles. To build a sandcastle, you only need a bucket and spade, but a plastic knife may help when doing the details.

First make your building surface as flat as possible. Be sure to choose a place far enough from the water so that your castle is not washed away each time the waves roll up the sand.

Remove any stray bits of rock, sea shells and seaweed from the sand. Put these to one side because you may want to use them later to decorate your castle.

Pack the sand firmly into the bucket to make your castle shapes. Keep the sand damp as you build or else your castle will start to crumble before you finish. If the tide starts to come in, you might have to build a wall around your castle. Some people make a moat around their castle. A ring of water around the castle makes it look more magical.

1. When you go to the beach to build a sandcastle, you should take

1. ________________ 2. ________________ 3. ________________.

2. The first step in making a sandcastle is to ______________________________

____.

3. To stop your castle from crumbling you should keep it ______________.

4. Write a rhyming word from *Building a Sandcastle* in the second box.

boat	
parcel	
bells	

5. Make a border design here using things you might find or see on the beach.

Understanding Descriptions

Descriptions play an important part in literary and factual material. They are useful in directions, in diaries, in travel brochures and when finding important details.

Descriptions are intended to let the reader share the writer's impressions. It is often said that descriptions are word pictures where the writer focuses on the detail.

If you enjoy riddles you should have no trouble with these exercises.

Read these descriptions and see if you can name the objects being described. Then draw a small picture in the space near your answer.

I have two hands. I have a round face. Sometimes I'm very noisy in the morning. I know my numbers from 1 to 12. I am a ______________________ .	I have a cap. I have a long neck. I am often clear in colour but sometimes I can be brown or green. I am useful when you are thirsty. I am a ______________________ .
I have four legs but no tail. Sometimes I'm a rectangle and sometimes I'm a circle. I'm found in the home but sometimes I am outside. It is at meal times most people find me useful. I am a ______________________ .	I have four wheels. I can only be used by one person a time. I should not be used on roads. I do not have an engine. My name has two parts. The first part rhymes with *gate*. I am a ______________________ .

Jan Weeks has used verse to give a description of a robot. She uses her character, Katie, to give the description. Katie's dog's name is Rufus.

Kzot the Amazing Robot

I saw a contraption, not very high —
It must have fallen right out of the sky.
Something alien to the human race —
Perhaps it had landed from outer space!
Its mouth was the shape of Rufus's bone
And its nose resembled an ice-cream cone.
It moved about on two very small legs,
The same shape and size as those old clothes pegs.
It had no body, just a square-shaped head.
It didn't have eyes — just flashing lights instead.
Antennae sprouted from either side
And instead of walking it seemed to glide.
'I'm Kzot!' it cried, 'I'm Kzot! I'm Kzot!
I am Kzot the amazing robot!'

1. Draw a line to match the part of Kzot's body with a shape.

legs	ice-cream cone
nose	square
mouth	dog's bone
head	clothes pegs

2. How tall do you think Kzot is? About ______________________________

3. Draw a picture of Kzot.

Living on Earth

by Colin Walker

People live on many different parts of the Earth's surface.
Some people live in houses built on the ice.
Some people live in tents on the sandy surface of the desert.
A long time ago, people used to live in caves that had rocky floors.
Homes give us **shelter**. Homes may be made of animal skins,

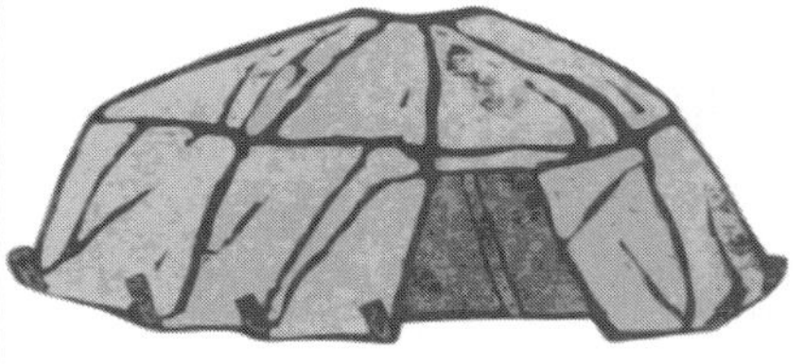

bark and branches,

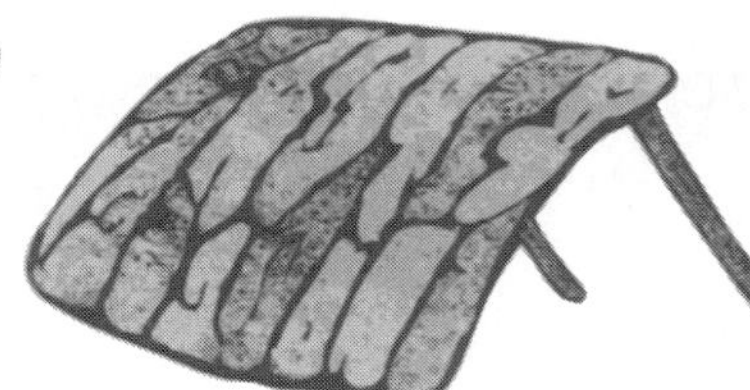

and bricks and timber.

Wherever people live, they always need a home that is close to food and water.

Complete these sentences.

1. Many people who live in deserts live in ______________________ .

2. A long time ago, people lived in ______________________ .

3. People build homes that are close to ____________ and ____________ .

4. Houses give people *shelter* from ______________________ .

5. Draw a picture of your home.

6. Write a sentence to describe your home. ______________________

____

Sometimes the reader may be asked to build up a description of a character from narrative writing.

It's so Hard to be Perfect

Samson was eight, the perfect age. He knew it was the perfect age because Galloping Grandpa told him so.

"If eight is the perfect age," he asked, as he rode his bike along beside Galloping Grandpa, who was training for the over-80s marathon, "then why aren't I perfect?"

"I think you're terrific," Galloping Grandpa puffed. "I wouldn't have you any different."

They turned the corner and started up the long slow hill which they used for training.

"But things are always going wrong," said Samson.

"You try your very best, don't you?" wheezed Grandpa.

"Yes," replied Samson, "but it never works out. Last week I took a tray of juice and toast to Mum on Sunday morning. She smiled, and because I was watching her smile, I tripped over her slippers and buttered toast landed on her head and juice went all over her bed."

1. Which word would you choose to describe Samson?

☐ perfect ☐ clumsy ☐ contented ☐ tired

2. Two words describe how Grandpa was breathing. What are those two words? ____________________ and ____________________

3. Samson was keeping up with Grandpa as they trained because he

(A) was riding his bicycle.
(B) was younger than Grandpa.
(C) had reached the perfect age of eight.
(D) had done more training than Grandpa.

4. Draw a line to complete each sentence correctly.

The buttered toast landed	all over the bed.
Samson had to ride	on Samson's mother's head.
The juice went	up a long hill.

Understanding Explanations

Explanations are an important factual text type. Scientific and technical explanations are often used to instruct students. Explanations are used in the exchange of information.

Of course, explanations can also be part of other text types. We often come across explanations in stories (narratives). In stories, explanations are usually less formal.

Explanations have been used in a number of other sections in this book.

Water

by Colin Walker

Most of Earth's surface is covered with water. Lakes, rivers, seas, oceans and ice cover about three-quarters of the Earth.

Most of the water on Earth is salt water. Some of the fresh water is in lakes, or rivers or in the air, but most of it is frozen as ice in the poles.

Rain comes from the water that is in the air.

Rain that falls on the land seeps underground or goes into rivers that flow into the sea.

The wind and the sun make the water **evaporate**. In the sky, the water vapour forms into tiny drops to make clouds. Eventually, it comes down again as rain.

1. Does this passage give the reader facts or opinions? ______________________ .

2. Water covers most of the Earth. ☐ True ☐ False

3. When we say water *evaporates* we mean it
(A) goes into the air.
(B) goes into rivers.
(C) turns into ice.
(D) goes underground.

4. Draw a picture to show a river running from the mountains down to the sea.

Put some clouds in your picture.

Add some rain.

Light

by Colin Walker

Most of our light comes from the sun.

Light from the sun travels through space and the air to Earth.

Light travels in straight lines.

Light can travel through water. When we swim we can see the end of the pool. If we are fishing, we may see the fish and the fish may see us.

Light can travel though some solid things too. These things we call **transparent** (see-through).

Light travels through glass and many plastics.

Light from the sun is white light. It is made up of all colours. Rainbows are made when raindrops separate the light into its colours.

The colours of the rainbow are red, orange, yellow, green, blue, indigo and violet.

1. Light is made up of many ______________________ .

2. Can you complete this table? There are many different things for each list.

Things that are transparent	Things that are NOT transparent

3. Draw a rainbow here.

   Put the colours in order.

   The red is on the top.

4. Light can travel through solid objects. ☐ True ☐ False

Extension — Cloze Exercises

The cloze exercises in this section require advanced reading and comprehension skills (see Understanding Questions, p. 18). The exercises use a variety of text types: folk tales, poetry, simple sentences, 'research' type text and fictional writing. The exercises include a variety of formats in order to make the student familiar with a wide range of cloze situations. Some exercises will be based on the understanding of grammar, while others require an appreciation of content and tone.

Remember: in cloze exercises you have to fill in the blanks — close the gaps — by choosing the best word to complete the passage.

1. These are the words that will complete the first passage.

years	were	women	drinks	deep	tombs

Write one word in each space.

Pharaohs

Pharaohs were the kings or rulers of Ancient Egypt. Pharaohs lived thousands of ______________ ago. They were so powerful people thought they ______________ gods. When Pharaohs died they were buried ______________ inside the giant pyramids. Pyramids were royal tombs built to protect the body of the Pharaohs.

Ancient Egyptians believed that a person needed food, ______________ and gifts for their life after death.

Pharaohs were buried with gold and other fine treasures. This is why so many ______________ were broken into many years later.

Very few ______________ ever became Pharaohs.

Choose the best word to complete the sentences from the words listed below. Underline the correct word — do not write in the spaces.

Lost Shoes

When Jenny woke up, she knew she had to get dressed quickly. Today she was going with (1) ______________ parents to the airport. Aunty Anne, her mother's sister, was coming to stay (2) ______________ them for a week.

Jenny put on her good clothes. She (3) ______________ her white socks with the small blue bows.

But she couldn't find her shoes.

She (4) ______________ under the bed. All she found were her slippers. She couldn't wear those to the airport!

She looked in the bathroom. (5) ______________ she found were her thongs. She couldn't wear those to the airport!

Where were her shoes? Then she remembered. She rushed out to the laundry to where she had (6) ______________ her sports bag.

Her shoes were still there, wrapped up in her towel.

1. (A) his
(B) her
(C) their

2. (A) at
(B) with
(C) beside

3. (A) found
(B) carried
(C) washed

4. (A) hid
(B) slept
(C) looked

5. (A) All
(B) How
(C) When

6. (A) made
(B) found
(C) left

7. In this exercise you have to work out the best word to fill the space in each sentence.

(A) Ashley and Simone ______________ playing basketball now.

(B) "Get out of my pool!" ______________ Mr Green angrily.

(C) When Tom's mother read his school report she was ______________ pleased with the excellent progress he had made.

(D) Carla ______________ her coloured pencils. She was sure she had lost one.

Choose the best word for each space. Circle the correct letter in the lists — do not write in the spaces.

A French Folk Tale

Once upon a time there lived a poor, poor woman call Truhana. Every year, about the same time, she went to the village market to **1.** ________ the honey she had collected from her beehives.

As she walked _ **2.** ________ the dusty road, carrying the jar of honey on her head, she tried to calculate how much money she would get.

"First of all, I will sell the honey," she thought, 'and with the **3.** ________ I get I will buy five eggs. I will set the eggs under one of my big brown hens. I will wait for the eggs to hatch." And she thought of the fluffy yellow chickens and smiled.

Then she thought, "When the chickens have grown I will buy some little white lambs."

Then Truhana dreamed how she could buy and sell, buy and sell, until she was rich. She would be **4.** ________ than all her neighbours.

1.	**2.**	**3.**	**4.**
(A) sell	(A) past	(A) eggs	(A) richer
(B) buy	(B) around	(B) honey	(B) bigger
(C) find	(C) along	(C) chickens	(C) older
(D) collect	(D) through	(D) money	(D) wiser

Choose the word for each numbered space from the lists on the next page. Circle your choice.

The Kowari

The *Kowari* is a kind of mouse. It is about the same size as a large rat and can be mistaken for one — at first glance. **5.** ________ it does have an unusual tail. It has bristly black hairs on the end which make a kind of brush.

The Kowari lives in Australia's rocky desert areas where it can get very **6.** ________ during the day. To escape the heat it digs burrows. It comes out at dusk to feed, when the day is cooler.

The Kowari is rather fierce. It **7.** ________ on small mammals, reptiles and insects which come out at night. It can **8.** ________ kill small chickens which makes it an enemy of the farmer.

5. But, Yet, Although, While

6. tired, worried, hot, sick

7. tames, feeds, avoids, helps

8. friends, sense, time, easily

9. This time write the answers on the lines. Choose the words from the list next to the passage. Cross each word out as you use it.

Suddenly the night was filled with a dreadful sound. It was a little like the screeching of car brakes, a spitting fire and the deep rumbling of ____________ . It was a wild, alien sound.

Pronto, the cat, nearly ___________ off the balcony ledge where he was sleeping. Peering down to the ground below, Pronto saw a huge, __________ face with ragged whiskers and eyes like orange traffic lights, claws as ____________ as barbed wire and teeth as dangerous as the teeth of the meanest ___________.

Worse still, she __________ Belinda's pet rabbit just in front of the snarling demon. The rabbit was so terrified it couldn't __________ . It didn't even twitch its nose.

fell
move
thunder
sharp
shark
ugly
saw

10. Use the words next to the poem to fill the spaces.

Autumn Leaves

by Aileen Fisher

One of the nicest beds I know
isn't a bed of soft white snow,
isn't a __________ of cool green grass
after the noisy mowers pass,
isn't a bed of yellow hay
making me itch for half the _________ —
but ___________ leaves in a pile that's high,
and deep and autumn-smelling, and dry.
That's the bed __________ I'd like to lie
and watch the flutters of autumn go by.

where
autumn
day
bed

Reading Poetry

Read this poem about children at the beach and answer the questions.

The Picnic

by Dorothy Aldis

We brought a rug for sitting on,
Our lunch was in a box.
The sand was warm. We didn't wear
Hats or shoes or socks.
Waves came curling up the beach.
We waded. It was fun.
Our sandwiches were different kinds.
I dropped my jelly one.

1. Many poems use rhyming words.

What words has the poet used to rhyme with: box? ______________

fun? ______________

2. Write two words that rhyme with beach. ____________ and ____________

3. What did the children have to eat on their picnic?

____

4. Some people may think the children were not properly dressed for the beach. They should have had their ____________ on.

Tick the answers for questions 5 and 6.

5. Jelly sandwiches were the only sandwiches the children had.

☐ True ☐ False

6. The sea was calm, with no waves. ☐ True ☐ False

7. Most families go to the beach in ____________________ .

8. Draw an under-the-sea scene across the bottom of this page.

The Swing

by Robert Louis Stevenson

How do you like to go up in a swing
  Up in the air so blue?
Oh, I do think it's the pleasantest thing
  Ever a child can do.

Up in the air and over the wall,
  Till I can see so wide,
Rivers and trees and cattle and all
  Over the countryside.

Till I look down on the garden green,
  Down on the roof so brown —
Up in the air I go flying again,
  Up in the air and down!

1. Name three things the child on the swing can see over the wall.

________________ ________________ ________________

2. What does the poet think is the most enjoyable thing a child can do? (Circle one letter.)

(A) climb a wall
(B) ride on a swing
(C) play in the garden
(D) walk in the countryside

3. In the poem, what do these colours describe?

blue ____________ green ____________ brown ____________

4. Find one compound word in the poem. ____________

5. Complete these lists with words from the poem that rhyme.

List 1		List 2	
countryside		do	
brown		thing	

I Keep Three Wishes Ready

by Annette Wynne

I keep three wishes ready
Lest I should chance to meet
Any day a fairy
Coming down the street.

I'd hate to have to **stammer**,
Or have to think them out,
For it's very hard to think things up
When a fairy is about.

And I'd hate to lose my wishes,
For fairies fly away,
And perhaps I'd never have a chance
On any other day.

So I keep three wishes ready,
Lest I should chance to meet
Any day a fairy
Coming down the street.

1. Who does the poet keep three wishes ready for? ____________________

2. The word *stammer* means to
(A) stamp your feet.
(B) stumble over your words.
(C) sound like a steam engine.
(D) forget what you were going to say.

3. If you have three wishes ready you don't have to ____________________.

4. If you don't have your wishes ready the fairy might ____________________.

5. Would you really expect to see a fairy walking down the street? __________

6. Which word does not rhyme with the other words in this list? Circle it.

street **foot** **Pete** **greet** **beat**

Upon the Beach

by Ilo Orleans

Upon the beach
With my **pail** and spade,
My sandy piles and wells I made.

And people passed
On every hand
And left their footprints in the sand.

Then came a wave
With the rushing tide —
And everything was washed aside.

1. What is another name for a *pail*?
(A) a hole (B) a wave (C) paint (D) a bucket

2. Draw pictures of the following objects:

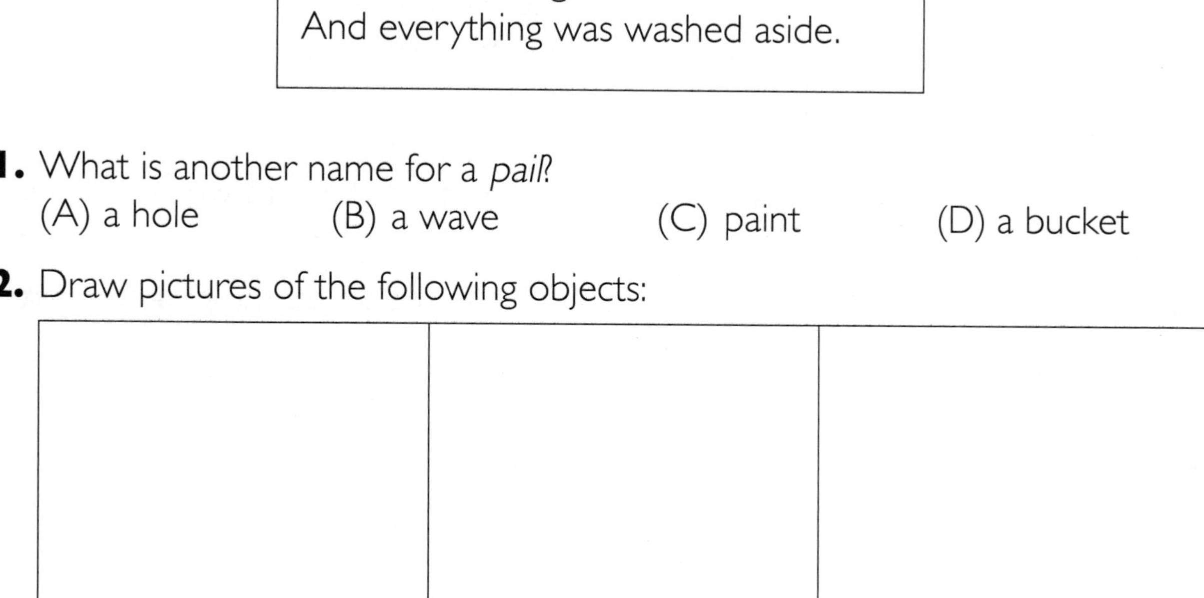

pail and spade	sandcastle	footprints

3. What do you like doing at the beach?

I like ______________________________________.

4. Draw a line to join words that rhyme.

spade	tide
wave	made
aside	brave

Appreciating Fables, Legends and Traditional Stories

Why the Numbat has a Red Back (a legend from Australia)

From ***Numbat, Run!*** by Jill Morris

Perentie the giant goanna and Walpurti the numbat were camping together in the desert.

They decided to paint pictures on each other's backs.

Walpurti took a stick and painted rings on Perentie's skin. Perenti painted stripes on Walpurti's fur.

Perentie was very pleased with the circles on his back, but Walpurti was **furious** when he saw the stripes Perentie had given him.

Walpurti picked up some red sand and threw it over his back.

The sand left a bright red blaze across the stripes.

That is why the numbat has a rusty-red blaze on its back, as well as stripes.

1. Before they painted each other's backs, the numbat and the goanna were

(A) lost. (B) friends. (C) enemies. (D) strangers.

2. The word *furious* could be replaced with the word

(A) *nervous.* (B) *furry.* (C) *angry.* (D) *excited.*

3. Do you think the numbat should have been upset with his stripes?

__________ Why do you think so? ____________________

____

4. The numbat painted the goanna's back first.

☐ True ☐ False

5. Name these animals.

________________ ________________

From *The Land of Ikaros* (a myth from Greece)

by Petro Alexiou

(This legend begins when Dedalos and his son, Ikaros, are held prisoners in a maze by King Minos. Dedalos had built the maze but he no longer knew the way out.)

There was no escape for Dedalos and Ikaros.

The maze had high walls but had no roof. Day after day, Dedalos gazed at the sky trying to think of a way out. One day, as he watched some birds flying overhead, he suddenly had an idea. "If birds can fly, so can we," he thought.

Dedalos made two pairs of wings out of feathers and wax. Dedalos and Ikaros strapped the wings onto their shoulders and arms.

When the time came for them to escape, Dedalos warned Ikaros, "Whatever you do, you must not fly too close to the sun or the sea."

Then at last they flapped their wings and rose out of the maze. They flew high into the sky and out over the sea. They were free.

The higher Ikaros flew, the more he enjoyed the feeling of flying. Forgetting his father's warning, Ikaros flew higher and higher into the sky.

Dedalos shouted to him to stop, but **in vain** — Ikaros could no longer hear him. Ikaros soared higher and higher, closer and closer to the burning sun.

Suddenly Dedalos saw feathers floating in the air about him. It was too late. The sun had melted Ikaros's wings and he fell from the sky into the sea.

Dedalos wept tears of grief for his son, but he continued on his flight . . .

1. Ikaros listened to his father's advice.

☐ True ☐ False

2. Circle one word to complete the sentence.

When Ikaros lost his wings he fell into the (**maze** **prison** **sea**).

3. When we say something is done *in vain*, we mean

(A) it was against the rules.

(B) it should not have happened.

(C) people had not thought about it.

(D) doing it didn't make any difference.

The Pied Piper of Hamelin

by Robert Browning

Many years ago, Robert Browning wrote the poem, *The Pied Piper of Hamelin*, which is based on a German legend. Here is part of his poem.

Rats!
They fought the dogs, and killed the cats,
They bit the babies in the cradles,
And ate the cheese out of vats,
They licked the soup from the cooks' own ladles,
Split open kegs of salted sprats,
Made nests inside men's Sunday hats,
And even spoilt the women's chats
By drowning their speaking
With shrieking and squeaking
In fifty different sharps and flats.

1. Which word would you choose to describe the rats? (Circle one.)

cute **shy** **bold** **cuddly** **scared** **feeble**

2. The rats spoilt the women's chats by ____________________

______________________________.

3. Find four words in the verse that rhyme with *rats*.

1	2	3	4

4. How would you feel if you met one of these rats? ____________________

____

5. What do you think was the worst thing the rats did? ____________________

____

Reading Picture Narratives

Stories can be told with pictures. A popular way of telling stories with pictures is in a comic strip. Most creators of comics try to use as few words as possible. They let the pictures tell the story.

Look at this short comic strip. We see John going to the school canteen. Speech is usually in speech bubbles. Each new picture is called a frame. Note: speech bubbles do not use speech marks (" ").

Comic strip characters often have very big features, such as large noses. Comic strips often have unexpected endings. This makes them funny.

1. How many frames are there in the comic strip above? ________________

2. It comes as a surprise (frame 4) to readers when they see the frog is
(A) eaten. (B) alive. (C) chocolate. (D) green.

3. What do you notice about John's shoes? They are ________________.

4. Read the fable 'The Lion and the Mouse' on page 24 and retell the story as a comic. You do not have to use all the frames. Write your name after *by* in the first frame.

The Lion and the Mouse by ________	**1**	**2**	**3**
4	**5**	**6**	**7**

Many Sunday newspapers have comics that publish children's photos.

Smile — CLICK!

This is my little sister Loren. She is 3 years old. Loren likes to play with our little brother, Harley. They climb on the stairs. Her favourite TV show is 'Bananas in Pyjamas'. She has their songs on a CD.

Hi, my name is Bindi. I live in the Blue Mountains. We have a lot of bush near our house. I like to go bushwalking and swimming in our dam. I want to be a ballet dancer when I grow up.

Hi! My name is Holly. I have a pet cat called Claws. I would rather have a horse, but we don't have enough room for a horse. Most of the time I like school but I don't like sport on very hot days.

1. Why do you think this part of the Sunday comics is called

Smile — CLICK!? ______________________________

2. Which person did NOT write her own letter? ______________________

3. Bindi was probably (**happy** **angry**) when this picture was taken.

4. In this space draw your own picture (or paste in your photo). Write a little bit about yourself that you would like to send to ***Smile*** — **CLICK!**

____

____

____

____

Interpreting Notices

When interpreting notices the student has to consider both the graphics and the text. Notices can range from the purely informative (*Snow Gum School Notice*) to the 'attention catching' (*Pet Search*). Students should look at words in large print but also search out any relevant detail. Dates are often important on notices.

Judy was given this notice at school to take home to her parents. They have to choose a sport for when Judy goes into Year 3.

Snow Gum School — Summer Sports Program

Dear parents,
Please read the information and fill in the form below.
Return the form to the school before Tuesday, 25 November.

Summer Sports — Term 1

Learn to Swim – All non-swimmers must do this sport.
Netball – (Year 3 to Year 6) girls only.
T-Ball – (Year 3 students only) boys and girls mixed.
Cricket – (Year 5 and Year 6 only) boys and girls. Limit 25 students.
Most matches will be played on the oval next to the school.
There will be one Saturday morning match against Craiglen, in Craiglen.
All cricketers should be available for this **annual** match.
Gymnastics – (Year 6 students only) In Sports Club Gymnasium.

- -

To the Sports Co-ordinator,
My ________________ , ________________, in Year ________ would like to
son/daughter name
do ________________ for their sport in Term 1.
first choice

1. Judy is going into Year 3. If Judy can swim, which sports can she choose as her summer sport? ☐ netball ☐ T-ball ☐ gymnastics

2. Which sport is for girls only? ________________ (A short answer is required.)

3. Which word would best replace the word *annual*?
☐ *long* ☐ *yearly* ☐ *normal* ☐ *important*

4. The form must be returned to the school by ________________.

5. Which sport does the school treat as very important?________________.

Read this notice and answer the questions.

1. The pet that was lost was a ________________. Its name was ________________.

2. What should you do if you find the lost pet?

- ☐ Ring Pet Search.
- ☐ Keep it.
- ☐ Tell the owner.
- ☐ Contact the police.

3. Circle the three things that would best help you recognise Sam.

age **colour** **ears** **tail** **hair** **collar**

4. The photograph is a picture of Sam. ☐ True ☐ False

5. How old was Sam when he was lost? ________________________